to Steve and Jeannine

The Delusion of Progress

All the Best!

Irresponsibly yours

Pierre

Sept. 2008

The Delusion of Progress:

A Fallacy of Western Society

SPECIMEN

Pierre A. Chomat

Translated from the French by
Victoria Dare

Universal Publishers
Boca Raton

The Delusion of Progress: A Fallacy of Western Society

Universal Publishers
Boca Raton, Florida • USA
2008

ISBN-10: 1-59942-986-1/ISBN-13: 978-1-59942-986-1 (*paper*)
ISBN-10: 1-59942-985-3/ISBN-13: 978-1-59942-985-4 (*ebook*)

www.universal-publishers.com

Cover illustration by Pierre Chomat

Library of Congress Cataloging-in-Publication Data

Chomat, Pierre, 1932-
  [Où va l'humanité? English]
  The delusion of progress : a fallacy of Western society / Pierre A.
  Chomat ; translated from the French by Victoria Dare.
     p. cm.
  Includes bibliographical references and index.
  ISBN 1-59942-986-1 (alk. paper)
  1. Social evolution. 2. Social problems. 3. Social change. 4.
  Civilization, Modern. 5. Materialism--Social aspects. I. Title.
  HM626.C457 2008
  303.44--dc22

                              2008015023

To the youth
Who will remedy the damage
That Western excess
Has inflicted on the world

And to Monix

The Delusion of Progress

A Fallacy of Western Society

Contents

Foreword

Our industrial society is insatiable. To stay on track it is depleting all valuable natural resources existing on our planet. Nevertheless we still believe that we will always be able to forge ahead. We are convinced that nothing can stop Progress.

As a result, we are on the brink of seriously destabilizing life on Earth. But we prefer to ignore the signs rather than imperil our sacrosanct economy. We have faith in Development.

If out of curiosity we dare to question the health of Western society – rumours imply a possible planetary crisis – we do not allow our thoughts to dwell on it very long and we rapidly deny facts that could suggest a disaster of that magnitude.

Finally, we, "developed people," seem not to care for the future of humanity. How can we be so blinded by our faith in Progress that we do not even want to know where we are collectively heading?

Pierre Auguste Clouet

By erasing God we placed ourselves face to face with reality.
How will it be when we have erased reality?

Jean Baudrillard[1]

PART I

DEVELOPMENT TO EXCESS

CHAPTER I

Why Development ?

The term fundamentalism is generally understood as the strict observance of fundamental doctrines and rituals of a religion. But it can also have a more general meaning outside the spiritual world. The American Heritage Dictionary extends the notion of fundamentalism to "a belief that does not rest on logical proof or material evidence" and Merriam-Webster's New Collegiate Dictionary to "a movement or attitude stressing strict and literal adherence to a set of basic principles."

I maintain that in industrialized countries people by and large have become fundamentalists of Progress.

By the middle of the 18th century, Western society was entering what it would later proudly call its Industrial Revolution. Along the way, it acquired the belief that scientific and industrial developments are beneficent because they bring Progress to all of humanity. Every action undertaken by science and technology paves the road of Progress. The two world wars of the last century drew most of their dreadful force and Machiavellian mechanisms from industrial development, but that did not deter people from the idea that, on the whole, industrial development is building the future of humanity. We are certain that we "progress" as surely as we breathe.

Under these conditions, one might think that Western society should have at least taken the precaution of defining the ultimate goals of Progress and then, from time to time, of checking to see if we are on track to achieving them. But it has not. Our goals are in Progress itself. We take for granted that Progress characterizes Man and that it is an unstoppable component of his being. Consequently, we do not, as a rule, check if our developments generate any collateral damage. When we do discover some, it is often after the fact and too late to correct anything.

We have faith in Progress. We do not question its value. Progress "exists" the way God "exists."

Before I began to immerse myself in technological development, I was lucky enough to discover an excellent professor of philosophy. According to him, "Philosophy was not just the domain of philosophers; science and industry also played a philosophical role in our world and have had an indelible impact on humanity. For more than a century, as industry shaped society, it had a major influence on Western civilization. It had more power over the evolution of our society than the finest discourses of the greatest thinkers." I had difficulty understanding his message. The thoughts of Auguste Comte or Immanuel Kant impressed me more than learning how engines could influence our way of thinking. Nevertheless, at the time, I assumed that I had grasped the essence of Mr. Cecconi's teaching, but in reality it was not until many years later that I came to more fully comprehend his sound assertions.

In 1975, I was offered a position in Iran as representative of a French engineering company. In the 1970s, Iran and Brazil were the two "developing" countries with the brightest future. Or, at least this was what the Western world liked to say, enamored as it was with transferring its technology to "less developed" countries. The Shahinshah of Iran, His Imperial Highness Mohammed Reza Pahlavi, wanted to westernize his country, although he also used to his advantage the aura of the great Persian emperors of the distant past. I immediately accepted the offer as I was eager to participate in the "development" of a country that held the promise of so bright a future.

For three years I was involved with everything that might advance Iran's industrial development, which was mainly geared towards the exploitation of hydrocarbons. My enthusiasm for industrial development seemed unshakeable when, suddenly, I realized that something was not quite right. I did not understand the deeper significance of the projects that I was promoting. I needed to understand what was really meant by the term "development." Why "develop?" Why "develop" Iran?

This revelation – for that is what it was – did not really come from within me. It originated in the streets of Tehran in the spring of 1978, when the people began to revolt against the Shah. It was the third time that I had seen a population mobilize to free itself of its Western yoke. As a young student on a summer internship in a phosphate mine in Morocco, I had been held captive for four days in a village besieged by Moroccans rebelling against French colonization. Later, in Algeria, during the long months of my military service, I witnessed a particularly tragic war of independence. Perhaps this was why, when in 1978 I sensed the birth of the revolutionary movement in Iran, I began to see my role in a new light.

At that time, the Shah ruled Iran under an authoritarian regime, forcing the people to adopt a Western mode of "development." He had effectively subjugated Iran to the West. Suddenly, the Iranian people no longer wanted to obey their monarch. The streets, the bazaar, the university in Tehran were filled with crowds ready to die to obtain their country's independence. The Iranian people did not want a way of life based on foreign values that were irrelevant to them and which, so far, had brought nothing but corruption from those in power. I saw the determination with which a whole people were prepared to face the fearsome royal army, which had always fired without hesitation on demonstrators in the bazaar when the occasion arose. I realized that the situation was serious. There was no longer any doubt that our type of society which was being imposed on the Iranians went against the very core of their being.

It was then that I realized that the mode of Progress, which characterizes Western societies and which the Shah wanted to impose on his subjects, was not universal. This created an abstruse doubt in me that I could not ignore. I started to examine what Development and Progress, as understood in "developed countries," really entailed.

This was the beginning of a long period of reflection. Today, I know that we, in the West, have let ourselves be carried away by our own enthusiasm. We are unable to sustain the civilization in which we have placed such hope. Incapable of curbing our momentum, we have not just exceeded our own development capacities but, far more seriously, we have exceeded the physical capacities of the earth to sustain our Development without disrupting the equilibrium on which we depend.

This book is the expression of that reflection. It takes some difficult paths, and some passages are as steep as the rocky ridges that only seasoned climbers undertake. I make no concession in it to those who, like me, have passionately pursued excessive industrial development. But beyond this reproach, I have tried to understand why, as a general rule in the countries that chose the industrial path, we did not first take the precaution of trying to find out where our actions will ultimately lead.

Why Development? This is really one huge "Why?"

CHAPTER 2

Do We Still Exist ?

I have embraced Development. I can only comprehend Progress from my own Western perspective. It troubles me to know that I have little chance of understanding people who have not adopted the Western way of life. It bothers me even more to know that I cannot perceive where industrial society is heading. I have been shaped by the society I was born into and no matter what I do, I cannot break free from it. So far, the mountains have offered me the best opportunity for escape.

I have a particularly vivid memory of one of my last visits to the French Alps a few years ago. It had been a rather gloomy winter in Paris and a longing to get out of town had led me high in the mountains, where industry had not yet forced its way.

The first morning I hiked beyond the cliffs to the upper plateau that I wanted to reach. At the end of a long rocky path, an exquisite carpet of spring flowers awaited me, as if laid there by the magic of time. Patches of snow still lingered just above, so these beauties could only have emerged from their winter slumber at most a few days before. Wild pansies in various colours spread out in little groups like swarms; some were mauve, others violet, or violet with a dab of yellow. Gentians also filled the scene and some had brazenly penetrated right to the heart of the most compact groups of pansies to unfurl their deep blue petals. Other flowers too had made their spring début and their many heads gleamed in the sunlight; but it was the pansies that impressed me most.

I found them slender and fragile, and both proud and humble at the same time. There was something in their nature that intrigued me, so I bent down to take a closer look. The long, thin grasses of the previous year, matted to the ground over the long winter months under the heavy blanket of snow, were wrapped around them in a carpet of a soothing grey. The leaves of the pansies had not yet had time to form; with no other vegetation to accompany them, the flowers looked as if they had been planted there by Fate. Perhaps because of that I found something abnormal about their situation, something even rather disturbing. I could not understand how they could be so fearless and serene because there were risks all around. I myself represented such a risk, and close by, there must be some little rodent, just out of hibernation, longing to curb its hunger. Should it appear, these flowers would have no chance of escape. They were there now and that was all that mattered. That evening they would lower their heads to the ground and the following morning raise them again to the sky. What a lesson in serenity!

The land was rugged with awe-inspiring slopes. Lower down, across the valley, a small village pressed against the hillside as if hunkered down against the rigors of winter. Rows of narrow terraces, built one above the other, in an attempt to grow a few crops, surrounded it. About four hundred years before, Huguenots had sought refuge on this mountain, as it was almost inaccessible to the dragoon corps who were hounding them in the valleys. Swollen with these immigrants, the village must have been forced to build higher terraces on slopes even more difficult to cultivate. My walk along the mountain path gave me plenty of time to appreciate the effort involved in creating these terraces. The result was impressive. The farmers of those days must have labored year after year to build the numerous little walls and to cultivate their tiny plots. It struck me that the villagers of that time were connected to the soil, just like my little flowers. Both had this in common: they were part of the land on which they depended for their very existence. As I contemplated the terraces, I felt a profound admiration for those who had toiled so hard to work the land.

Having spent my whole adult life traveling from one venture to the next, I could not help but compare my lot in life with that of the old mountain-dwellers. I belong to an itinerant world, to a world that no longer needs to ground itself in order to subsist, a society that can no longer appreciate the nature, which forms the very essence of its existence; a society in which people, little by little, have become rootless.

What a difference between men now, trying to surround themselves with a little more technology every day, and men then, who, like the mountain flowers, adapted themselves to nature, despite the often harsh adjustments that it demanded of them. Up there on the little plateau, I soon felt out of place. I even felt somewhat uneasy, almost as if I did not exist. At that moment, I was convinced that we do not truly exist if we do not recognize ourselves in the midst of other beings and all other forms of life, and our relations and responsibilities toward them. We lose all sense of existence when we are totally detached from nature; we simply no longer exist in the real sense of the word.

I knew that after leaving that haven of tranquility, I would go back to the world of the villagers below, down where the road began. After crossing the bridge over the stream, I would come to the first garbage dump that the village had set up just beside the stream. I had discovered it that morning, before taking the mountain path. A man whom I had met near the dump had told me that he came from time to time to set fire to it. He was convinced that what goes up in smoke is gone forever and he seemed to derive from his work the impression of a job well done. He also arranged for the garbage that could not be burned to be washed "out of sight" by the stream during the heavy rains.

As I thought about this first befouling of nature, I felt ashamed to look again at my little flower friends. I knew that I would go back down the path to where I had left my car. Then, comfortably ensconced in my steel box, I would drive back down the winding road leading to the large valley and then, further down, on to the big cities, on big roads, full of cars, full of trucks, loaded with the manufactured products of men. I would push my internal-combustion engine to go at the speed of the valley-dwellers. I would drive into the plumes of smoke rising from the steelworks built alongside the mountain waterfalls; I would inhale the mixture of gases served by the towns for us to breathe; and suddenly, I would have the sensation of being back at factories made of metal, glass and concrete, and vast refineries with gleaming aluminum-colored pipes. My world. The world in which, for years on end, I had gained so much satisfaction as I actively participated in the construction of industrial systems.

On my way down the mountain, I took the opportunity to take another look at the rows of terraced fields, which were almost all abandoned now. When I arrived at the little village, a poster depicting a white minibus, mounted on tracks and gliding across the snow like a magic sleigh, caught my eye. It said that next winter, this new marvel of the slopes would take tourists up to an elevation of 12,000 feet (3,600 meters), to the foot of some of the most magnificent peaks in the Alps.

It was probably going to ride over my mountain flowers. It might even run on fuel from one of the refineries that I had helped build.

CHAPTER 3

Our Ego-Systems

Not everyone on earth gets the chance to go and see the flowers of the mountains or the meadows. Young people born in a megalopolis like Tokyo, Sao Paolo, Bombay, Mexico, New York or Hong Kong often have no inkling about the role of nature in human life. For them, the environment is made up of concrete, steel, asphalt and waste. It is culturally impossible for them to imagine that any other type of environment might exist outside their own world. Of course, from time to time they might see pictures of graceful animals in verdant grasslands, but to them these images of natural life are just a few more advertisements or pictures in a book.

Yet, throughout the history of Man, since hominids first began walking on two feet around five million years ago, more than ninety-nine percent of Man's time on earth has been spent in nature. People did not shut themselves away in cities until much later, a mere ten thousand years ago in the first cities of Mesopotamia. It was still thousands of years more before they would pack themselves together in large cities and only in the last few centuries in megalopolises. Despite the shortness of time spent in towns and suburbs, we have, for the most part, so profoundly adapted to urban life that we often barely see the importance of nature's equilibrium. Unless we actually bother to think about it, we just assume that the material environment in which we find ourselves today can support life by itself. We have learned to live in dead spaces.

The children of the mega-cities are not the only ones to overlook nature's existence. The industrial world is even more prone to forget it. It has adopted the humanist philosophical concept of the Greek Seneca who, in the first century AD, placed the human being at the center of existence: "Man is something sacred for man." Industrial society is still not ready to admit that ecosystems form the basis of life on earth and that they have to be protected before Man himself.

Ecosystems do not have specific boundaries. Small eco-systems are part of larger ones, which are part of even larger ecosystems, and so on all the way up to the great ecosystem, Planet Earth. At first glance, ecosystems may seem simple, but in reality they are complex and very fragile. They are so intricately interwoven that it would be very difficult to know where one leaves off and the next one begins. Only nature can tell.

An ecosystem is an assemblage of plants, animals and other living organisms living together within their environment, evolving and functioning as a dynamic and complex whole. But this beautiful assemblage is delicate and can easily be shattered. When a chain of actions is broken, the ecosystem must readapt, but it is not always able to do so. Some ruptures are irreversible. If a species disappears, it affects not only the species that had fed on it, but also those on which it fed, those with whom it had lived in symbiosis, those that had recycled its waste...

Within this living dynamic world based on interdependence, harmony and delicacy, industrial society has set up "ego-systems." "Ego-systems," to be sure, are very different from ecosystems. Unlike natural ecosystems, in which everyone finds a place in the circle of life, ego-systems have room for only one dominating species: Man and they are designed to serve only his interests. As for the other species and their habitats, those that get in his way are eliminated; those that offer some advantage are domesticated or consumed.

An ego-system is not designed to operate over generations as farms once were. Instead, it is organized to profit as quickly as possible from the natural resources it exploits with little concern for their depletion or effect on the environment. The "underdeveloped" peoples that are exploited by the "developed" ones can also be counted as natural resources.

The objectives of ego-systems are money and power. Ego-systems control the sectors that they have chosen to exploit. Agro-industry is a good example of an ego-system. The pharmaceutical industry is another. Medicine can effectively cure many diseases but the human body only retains a small portion of most of the drugs it takes in. Most of the pharmaceuticals that we ingest are excreted and end up in rivers, and very likely in the oceans, where they affect other forms of life. National drug administrations control the research and production of medicines in order to protect their country's citizens, but they very rarely take into consideration the damage that the products cause in nature.

As with ecosystems, the interplay of competition, predation, parasitism and mutualism also exists in ego-systems but in the case of the latter, ego-systems are always directed to benefit Man. They strengthen Man's superior position.

Our species has long demonstrated its skills, passion and zeal for drawing on the resources of the earth, be they animal, vegetable, or mineral. The arrival of motors that run on fossil fuels was a godsend for us. It allowed us to methodically exploit the riches of our planet far beyond the areas naturally accessible to us. Before large-scale use of energy, our methods of exploiting these resources still had a human dimension: the first whale hunters went to sea rowing their boats; fur-trappers went about on foot. The use of non-human energy allowed Man to transform his activities into industrial exploitation.

An edifying example of overuse of energy for the benefit of Man is the commercial sardine fishing that began at the beginning of the last century in Monterey Bay in California, and which I describe in *Oil Addiction: the World in Peril.*[2] This fishery might have lasted if it had kept the family-run character of its roots. With motorized boats and mechanization, how-ever, it rapidly became an industry. Soon, the boats no longer had to return to quay to be unloaded; the sardines were pumped straight from buoys in the sea into the canneries that lined the shoreline for almost a mile. This industrial exploita-tion demonstrated its destructive effects when it began turning the fish that could not be absorbed by the food market into agricultural fertilizer. At this point, the ego-system had become unstoppable. In the season of 1936-37 alone, more than two hundred thousand tons of sardines were reduced to fertilizers and other chemicals in this way, almost twice the amount that were put in cans. Clearly the economic interests of the com-pany took precedence over any other consideration. The sardine ego-system of Monterey Bay was stopped only by the disappearance of the sardine shoals themselves.

The twentieth century businesses that have remained profitable have almost all given rise to scientifically organized industrial ego-systems, all of which are bent on the total exploitation of nature's valuable resources. Energy and tech-nology are cleverly allied to force nature through the Caudine Forks[1] of increasingly powerful ego-systems. These ego-systems have invaded every area of activity: the production of civil and military infrastructure and equipment, the armed forces themselves, transport, agro-industry, fishing, public health, entertainment, education, media, etc. Together, they form an inextricable social and technological tangle in which each ego-system depends on numerous others. Industrialized societies claim, however, to have a highly laudable common goal that they choose to call Development.

Of course, some developments have highly laudable aims but researchers are paid with funds derived directly or indi-rectly from the exploitation of the planet. In our industrialized world, even salutary developments are often funded by the

---

[1] Caudine Forks (Furculae caudinae): two narrow wooded gorges meet in a pass near Caudium (east of Naples, Italy). In 321 BC, a Roman army of 40,000 men was trapped at the pass by the tribes of Samnium, with no way to escape.

ego-systemization of the earth's resources. There is a French proverb from Burgundy that says: "There is no front without a back." In other words, the enormous privileges that we enjoy today will not be without unpleasant consequences in the future.

CHAPTER 4

Insatiable Society

*I find on earth a greedy, insatiable, and relentless
man, who wants, at the expense of anything he
meets or finds in his way, and whatever it may cost
to others, to provide for himself alone, to swell his
fortune and to inundate himself with possessions.*

Jean de La Bruyère, 1688 [3]

Western Man did not delay in using his Industrial Revolution to pursue prosperity and power, but until the end
of the eighteenth century, he did so in a way that still left room
for hope that one day he would achieve and maintain a tenable
way of life.

In the beginning, no one suspected that industrialization
would lead to the development of a consumer society so insistent on excess. Voltaire believed that the growing industry
could be a force for good. "Industry has repaired all the
wrongs that nature and neglect have done to our country," [4] he
said. A century later, philosophical economists even saw in
industry a lever for social progress. Saint-Simon's doctrine of
industrialism[i], Charles Fourier's phalansteries[ii] and the Owenite

---

[i] Saint-Simon (1760-1825) French philosopher and economist. In *Le
catéchisme des industriels* (1823) industrialism is defined as a social philosophy
based on a religion of science. Saint-Simon's socialism was based on
technocracy and economic planning. He envisaged a nation organized like a

communities of Robert Owen[iii] were all inspired by this idea. At the end of the nineteenth century, the American theorist Edward Bellamy[5] still firmly believed that, before the year 2000, thanks to Progress, human beings would reach a level of development that would bring satisfaction to all. He thought that having reached this level of wellbeing, competition between humans would be neither needed nor sought.

We now know how utopian and quixotic these hopes have proved to be. The economists, sociologists and philosophers who believed that industrial development could satisfy once and for all the needs of individuals were mistaken. Our industrial development was launched on the basis of ill-founded ideals. In fact, industry, in order to maintain itself, must keep producing more and more and stimulate the population to raise its standard of living even to excess. It cannot content itself with serving people who, satisfied with their condition, no longer desire more. On the contrary, industry can only survive in countries whose society is structured to promote constant acquisition. In order to maintain sufficient levels of consumption by the population, corporations are condemned to constantly renew their products and technologies to create new desires. Industrialized society is forced into permanent growth. Just as pelagic sharks must keep moving in order to force the oxygen-bearing water over their gills, for to stop, is fatal.

There is however one crucial difference between the constant motion of the shark and of our society: the shark

---

vast workshop in which industry would be developed in the interests of all, without differences of birth, and where economic power would be entrusted to the industrialists.

[ii] Charles Fourier (1772-1837) French philosopher and economist. In *Le nouveau monde industriel et sociétaire* (1829) his phalansteries are described as small autonomous units of production and consumption in which the workers would live together as a community.

[iii] Robert Owen (1771-1858) Welsh pioneer in cooperative industry. His Owenites were cooperative communities for both production and consumption. He devoted all his time, and money, to promulgating his social doctrine in Great Britain and the US.

knows what speed will satisfy his oxygen needs; our society does not know its limits. In order to sustain itself, our society fosters a culture of insatiability. In fact, so far it has been the countries that have most intensely cultivated the insatiability of their citizens that have been the most successful economically. In the United States, creation and manipulation of desire by advertising has become a national cult in itself. It is so deeply integrated into the way of life that it is difficult to imagine how the country could function without it.

As contradictory as it may seem, in order for a free-market society to ensure that its economy will continue to satisfy the people, it must keep them in a perpetual state of dissatisfaction. While this dilemma remained within reasonable limits at the beginning of the twentieth century, it has since grown out of all proportion. A purely agricultural society, even a modern one, would probably have been able to find a balance, as this balance would have been imposed upon it by nature's capacity to produce. On the other hand, an industrialized society, condemned to always consuming more and more, is driven to exhaust the resources on which it is based. It cannot last.

At the very beginning of the Industrial Era, material "success" still depended on the physical effort exerted by humans and their draft animals. By introducing fossil fuels *en masse* into Man's activities, we have multiplied by thousands of times our own means of production. We are in a vicious spiral: "exploitation of resources → industrial production → consumption → exhaustion of resources" through which we are gradually digging the grave of industrial society. "Our own grave."

But how have we been able to indulge our insatiability so excessively without noticing the dangers? After all, we seem to have understood the principles of Jean-Jacques Rousseau. Rousseau believed that the conflict between Man and society could be a means of progress, with each benefiting from the other, as long as a *Social Contract* was respected: "What man loses by the social contract is natural liberty and an unlimited right to everything he tries to get and succeeds in getting; what he gains is civil liberty and proprietorship of all he possesses."[6] Unfortunately, in today's society, Rousseau's principles can only be adhered to with great difficulty. Some people even consider them to be the antithesis of Development. The culture of individual insatiability indulges individualism at the expense of pluralism; it feeds the conflict between individuality and plurality. Community spirit is sacrificed on the altar of consumption. Rousseau's *Social Contract* has become just another tricky subject with which to tax students in their university exams.

Long before Jean-Jacques Rousseau, Thomas Hobbes[7] sought to discover the way in which human beings could live together with dignity in society. He knew it would be difficult. But neither Hobbes nor Rousseau could logically have foreseen that the two partners, Man and society, would mostly act in concert on one point: the pillaging of nature to profit from its riches as quickly as possible.

Since the days of these social thinkers, industrialization has created a very different society than the one that they imagined. The drive to squander the earth's resources has not ceased to gain momentum. The first great industrial break-throughs led the more enterprising to believe that there were no limits, that nothing could bar the impossible. It is thus not surprising that the domestication of fossil energy was very quickly taken to be a providential means to push back the boundaries of the impossible. Every nation wishing to "develop" itself has exploited, to various degrees, the means offered to it by energy. Energy is used to satisfy the most excessive and often the most superfluous demands. In the United States, the size of many cars is so out of proportion to their purpose that one might believe that they were designed as engines primarily to produce CO_2.

We continue our vicious circle of Development as if natural resources were unlimited. The Development on which our industrialized society depends will seem to future generations much more like the development of a plan for eradication than the salutary advance of human beings. We in the West can no longer be proud of our "marvelous" Industrial Revolution. We have been unable to control it. Through pure vanity we have destroyed the hopes that once we were right to place in it.

By wasting it, we have betrayed the earth. We have betrayed it by stealth in the name of Progress, our own, for the "greatest happiness for the greatest number." We often have done so in the name of God, again our own. Today, this betrayal is global. In just a few centuries, we have reduced the earth from a natural state of being to an artificial one. We will need to answer for this to future generations.

For a long time, insatiability was considered to be a vice. The classical Greeks considered insatiability to be a moral fault going against restraint, moderation and sobriety. Even the Epicureans agreed on this principle, contrary to their reputation. "Epicurus emphasized that the pleasurable results of an action must always be weighed against its possible side effects."[8] The Greek philosophers must have had reasons for thinking so. It was not just a sacrifice they imposed on themselves to please their gods.

From Antiquity to the Enlightenment, insatiability was not tolerated except for the less virtuous kings, queens and emperors as their royal prerogative. Insatiability was the flame which maintained the ambition and arrogance of Cleopatra until her death: "... insatiable for pleasure, insatiable for riches, [she] often showed a laudable ambition and often also an arrogant disdain; she acquired the kingdom of Egypt through love and, having hoped to seize the Roman Empire by this means, she failed in the latter and lost the former. She captivated the two greatest Romans of her time and killed herself because of the third."[9]

We have democratized insatiability along with our society. Not only is insatiability not perceived to be a vice, on the contrary it is seen as a right that we should all exercise in order to maintain our countries' good economic health.

If, until the twentieth century, philosophers did not see that insatiability would become a phenomenon of society, this is not the case today. Dominique Quessada considers our society to be "autophagous": "In an auto-consuming society, the powerful media control [consumerism]. Publicity appears ... to be the discourse that is best suited to enable industry to manage society."[10]

Where then are our society's safety barriers? How will our leaders manage to contain our appetite when it has become imperative to do so? How will they manage to leave us some hope of sustaining our way of life? How will they use their celebrated economic policy, which is presented as a true science allowing economic planners to establish the optimum balance between the degree of abundance of resources and the desired objectives of the population? Could a better economic policy hold the key to our future salvation? Our present policy has itself been perverted from its social purpose. It only takes into account the natural resources that are available on the market and only very exceptionally considers their degree of depletion. For as long as fossil fuels remain on the market, even in small quantity, they will be treated as a substance to be exploited for profit.

Teddy Roosevelt had good reason to worry:

> *The nation behaves well if it treats the natural resources as assets which it must turn over to the next generation increased and not impaired in value.*
>
> *Teddy Roosevelt 1910*

CHAPTER 5

Pampered Beings

In 1750, people had recourse to the labor of draught animal for labor. I estimate that these animals enabled them to multiply fivefold their own physical capacity. At that time, there were only 660 million people on earth. If we consider their draught animals as "energy servants," with 5 for each person, they represented a force of about 3 billion human workers. Today the earth houses 6,600 million people. Instead of draught animals, they benefit from power derived mainly from hydrocarbon, nuclear and hydraulic sources. The amount of energy they consume is equal to the work of 30,000 billion energy servants – nearly 5,000 servants per person. In 250 years, world population has multiplied by a factor of 10, but over that same period the number of energy servants that the world employs each day has multiplied by a factor of 10,000.

I call our new energy servants "ergamines." *Ergon* in Greek means work, and *gamine* in French means young girl. The two words together are meant to imply that ergamines are like little Cinderellas working for us. (Appendix A compares the energy potential of an ergamine to that of a man). The number of ergamines employed today represents a stupendous increase in work capacity. The energy released by this army of forced workers no longer just performs work on earth; it is attacking the earth itself.

We have multiplied the number of energy servants through motors and chemicals so fast that we have lost control of our so-called Development. They transfer their immense power to ego-systems that have their own rules and that are not necessarily in the human interest.

Human activity is maintained by a steadily increasing number of ergamines. First prize goes to the United States. Americans alone use a quarter of the ergamines dedicated to transforming the globe into a gigantic ego-system. This equates to an average of more than 20,000 invisible ergamines that are burned each day to serve every single North American. This figure does not include the colonies of ergamines consumed for them in China, Thailand, India and other parts of the world nor the regiments of them that are drafted into the US armed forces assigned overseas. Even though Europeans and the Japanese have only half as many energy servants at their disposal, they still enjoy a more than royal service. It is unlikely that any of the princes, kings or emperors of the past ever had as many conscripted subjects at their service. Neither Pharaoh Akhenaton and Queen Nefertiti in their Egyptian Palace at Tell El Amarna, nor Darius the Great, the King of the Persians at Persepolis, nor Qin, the First Emperor of China, nor Catherine the Great of Russia in her splendid Summer palace near St Petersburg ever had at their disposal such an army of servants as those serving the average North-American, European or Japanese family today.

Thanks to these providential servants, those of us in the "developed" countries live in a luxury that we cannot even begin to appreciate. It is impossible for us to measure the excess of comfort that the majority of us enjoy. We lead a princely existence without even realizing it. Of course, the life of a prince in the past had many advantages, but no royalty ever had the opportunity of having science take care of his health; the Emperor Qin most likely died from drinking too much "mercury of life" prescribed to him by the imperial *archiater* to grant him immortality. None of them had the means of knowing instantaneously what was happening throughout their territory; Darius the Great only received news of his furthest satrapies from time to time and not all this news was reliable. None of these illustrious persons ever had the pleasure of flying over their kingdoms, even once, whereas now, at any time of day, there are more people in the air in planes than there are inhabitants of Iceland. After we are buckled into comfortable seats in a plane, we no longer wonder at the feat involved in allowing us to fly. It is as if flight were a natural function for us. Maybe we should remember the brave Icarus, who boldly took himself for a god. He realized too late that, despite wearing the finest wings in mythology, he was unable to remain airborne for long.

In industrialized countries, our lives are inextricably bound to technology. What we call "life" has nothing to do with natural existence, for Man today is merely functioning in a material, sometimes virtual, universe. We cannot imagine, for example, that, a plane traveling from San Francisco to Europe, will guzzle 500,000 ergamines for each of its passengers. A total of 500,000 for each and every one! This information is never communicated to us by those who know. It is unlikely that any airline flying between California and Germany would ever dare to print on the tickets of passengers a message such as this:

During your flight from San Francisco to Frankfurt this aircraft will burn a half ton of kerosene - just for you. If used for menial labor on land, there would be enough fuel to carry out the work of 500,000 laborers over the course of a whole day. We would also like to inform you that the airplane will discharge into the atmosphere, especially for you, one and a half tons of carbon dioxide. Fat free. Please note that this privilege, granted to each of our passengers, is just for a one-way trip.

It has been a pleasure having you fly with us and we hope to welcome you on board our planes soon in the future.

Signed: The Chairman.

We, the privileged inhabitants of the Western world, are pampered beings. We take cars or planes as easily as the under-privileged take their donkeys, if they still have one. We are devotees of technology. We have developed ego-systems that we now need to maintain if we want to keep our way of life. In fact, we have become subservient to them. We have mechanized our world through these ego-systems. We function more than we live.

CHAPTER 6

Ego-Systems Cover the Globe
The World is Theirs

C ontrary to what one might expect, ego-systems are not designed to safeguard the world of the living. Intensive energy consumption has given them such colossal power that they generate phenomena on a global scale as significant as some natural phenomena can be, like volcanism, earthquakes, cyclones or marine currents. Of course, for now, ego-systems ensure an easy life for those served, but they also impair life on earth. Mindless of anything but their own objectives of power, they proceed blindly. They do not care about the future, even not their own.

We can congratulate ourselves for the fact that the earth is definitely in our hands, but we may not be so smug for long.

The country with the most powerful ego-systems is the United States. Its politics of deregulation have allowed many American corporations to become so financially powerful that they are beyond the control of the federal administration itself, let alone a single state. ExxonMobil's total revenue for the year 2006 was in the order of $370 billion. This figure corresponds roughly, for the same year, to the annual national budget of France and almost three times the budget of California, the richest of the American states.

In 1911, the Supreme Court of the United States found that John D. Rockefeller's Standard Oil Trust, which by then held a 64% share of the US market in oil, had engaged in illegal monopoly practices and ordered that the Trust be broken up into thirty-four companies. In 1999, almost a century after this noteworthy event, the American Congress had no objections to the merger of two of the five most important of these very same companies deriving from the 1911 break-up, namely Standard Oil of New Jersey (Exxon) and Standard Oil of New York (Mobil) to create ExxonMobil.

American oil companies are not the only oil companies benefiting from gigantism. British Petroleum, a company founded in Persia under the British Empire in 1908 under the misleading name of the Anglo-Persian Oil Company, is similarly outsized. Its total revenue for 2006 of over $270 billion amounted to almost three quarters of the budget of England. Together, the international oil corporations have so much financial power that they influence, and very often guide, the foreign policy of almost every country. In fact, they shape the overall world economy.

For the past three decades, successive American governments in Washington DC were elected thanks to the strong financial backing of the major American industrial groups and particularly those who are directly or indirectly related to the energy and military ego-systems. This phenomenon recently reached such a critical level that the election that placed G.W. Bush in power in 2001 was in reality a grotesque parody of a country exercising universal suffrage. Today, the President of the United States is above all the spokesperson for the powerful American corporations and he only represents the citizens in a secondary capacity; this is ironic for a country claiming to be the model of democracy. In discussions in Washington DC, the economic health of the major corporations takes precedence over that of the population. It also takes priority over the problems of the States of the Union. In reality, some of the most important discussions that affect national decisions do not take place in Congress between elected representatives of the people but rather in the board rooms of big corporations.

This steering of politics has serious consequences. To communicate with supranational groups, the government has to rise to a supranational level and its priorities become those of powerful groups at the expense of the American people. It finds fallacious arguments to justify its policies that systematically favor the big corporations. Americans must content themselves with news that has been carefully distilled for them by the White House. With regard to foreign policy, the President also places himself above international bodies like the United Nations whose sessions he either uses to his advantage or ignores, depending on the interests of the moment. When the President goes to war, the Geneva Conventions, although signed by the United States, are no longer necessarily relevant. The Kyoto Protocol, which deals with the environment globally, seems not to apply to the United States – or rather, to American ego-systems. And to avoid any legal action against American politicians or those in its administration, the federal government does not recognize the International Court of Justice. American "exceptionalism" is the base of G. W. Bush foreign policy.

To stay in the economic race, the other industrialized nations follow the American movement. Ego-systems cover the globe. The world is theirs.

CHAPTER 7

Development to Excess

E xcessive and useless Development is threatening the sustainability of our society. Although it is easier today than in the past to identify the material developments leading to false progress, our governments continue to encourage them. Development of excess is the privilege of the powerful of the world. In 2005, Western Europe launched the largest passenger plane that has ever existed[i]. Little did it matter to the participating governments of France, Germany, Great Britain and Spain that, by encouraging more people to travel by air, they are indirectly exacerbating climate change on earth. Little did it matter to them if it accelerated the depletion of basic valuable resources. The USA is obviously not to be outdone. In March 2005, Sean Kay and Theresa Hitchens wrote that "The Bush administration is completing a new Presidential Decision Directive that would move the United States quickly into the uncharted territory of deploying offensive anti-satellite weapons and space-based weapons for attacking targets on earth."[ii] These two examples of excessive Development show

---

[i] The Airbus A380, which was presented at the 2005 Air show at Le Bourget, just north of Paris, is an airplane capable of transporting 800 passengers.

the casualness with which the leaders of industrialized countries treat the future. The future of our "civilization."

Immoderate developments arise every day in every field of activity, at every opportunity, and not just in the industrial domain. In 2007, there were 17,000 golf courses throughout the United States, and their number continues to grow at a rate of several hundred per year. Each of them requires a daily average of more than 50,000 gallons of water to keep the grass green. In comparison, an inhabitant of the Sahel, on the edge of the Sahara desert, has less than half a gallon of water a day to meet all his needs. Moreover, golf courses are not just sprayed with water but also with "an average of 18 pounds of pesticides per acre, per year" compared with an average of "2.7 pounds of pesticides per acre, per year, in agriculture."[12]

The consequences of our Development can be alarming. Our fragile world depends on a great balancing act to subsist in the form that we know. They are like knife slashes on the canvas of the biota, terrestrial and marine, which is already showing significant damage.

In this rush for Development, cities are clearly in the forefront. They have lost the harmonious proportions they once had and are now deformed by the excrescences of excessive Development. Pushing forward their boundaries by building ever more houses on their outskirts, they spill far into the countryside. In these extensions, nature has been "reordered" so as to accommodate people. Those who live there rarely move about on foot. When they do, it is on meticulously manicured and chemically maintained lawns. Urban industrial zones complete the scene. They represent totally dead spaces.

The large agricultural plains of the industrialized countries are in no better state. Agribusiness has descended on them with a vengeance. Their flat surfaces, which are ideal for exploitation on an industrial scale, now look more like construction sites than traditional farmland. Giant machines cruise around imperiously. The two vast Californian plains of the Sacramento Valley in the north and the San Joaquin Valley in the south are singular examples of industrialization to excess.

They form an immense agro-industrial ego-system functioning day and night for most of the year. Barely any native animal life remains and many crops have been drastically hybridized or genetically "enhanced." Intensive irrigation, industrial fertilizers and other chemical compounds have already altered the San Joaquin Valley to such an extent that a quarter of it is acknowledged to be uncultivable. In the same region, cattle no longer graze in pastureland. They are packed together by the tens of thousands into huge metal pens in which they are fed through programmed devices, sometimes through pipelines. Systematically treated with antibiotics and subjected to anabolic steroids, hormones and other biologically active agents to promote growth, they remain imprisoned there until they reach the economic weight required for selection for the slaughter house.

In the face of industry, the great forests have not fared any better. On the west coast of the United States, before the arrival of the European pioneers in the 1840s, there were more than three thousand square miles of virgin forest. Today only four and half per cent of this treasure remains intact. A few hundred giant trees have escaped the reckless saw of the lumberjacks. Some are more than two thousand years old, have a base sixteen feet in diameter and rise majestically to a height of three hundred and fifty feet. But even more surprising is the canopy. Springing from enormous branches extending horizontally high in the trees, there rises a second forest made up of hundreds of smaller trunks which, nevertheless, are particularly impressive. Richard Preston[13] gives a fascinating description of the biological richness of these redwood canopies that Steve Sillett[ii] has explored:

[ii] Steve Sillett, PhD in botany from Oregon State University in Corvallis, is one of the few scientists who are exploring the old-growth redwood forest along the coast of California and Oregon.

> The old-growth redwood-forest canopy ... is packed
> with epiphytes, plants that grow on other plants. ... There
> are hanging gardens of ferns ... [that] can weigh tons when
> they are saturated with rain-water; they are the heaviest
> masses of epiphytes which have been found in any forest
> canopy on earth. Layers of earth, called canopy soil, accu-
> mulate over the centuries on wide limbs and in the tree's
> crotches – in places where trunks spring from trunks – and
> support a variety of animal and plant life. ... Sillett and his
> students have found ... small, pink earthworms of an uni-
> dentified species, ... aquatic crustaceans called copepods
> [of an as yet unidentified species], ... wandering salaman-
> ders ... breeding in the redwood canopy, which suggests
> that they never visit the ground, ... thickets of huckleberry
> bushes with berries, ... currant bushes, elderberry bushes
> and salmonberry bushes ...

While we may be able to find some excuses for the pioneers who initially lumbered these redwood forests, the same
cannot be said now of those who still seek, by every imaginable
financial and political means, to cut down the few remaining
old growth trees in the region. The eradication of these pristine
forests, which is sought only for the purpose of extracting an
immediate profit, would destroy an extremely rich ecosystem
that is unique in the world and has required thousands of years
of tranquility to form. It is difficult to imagine that the last of
these trees could disappear before we can figure out by what
trick of nature their sap manages to rise to the very top of their
great height.

The United States is not the only country to extend ego-
systems to extremes. The pioneers from the Old Continent had
learned their lessons well before setting off for the Americas.
By then, the Europeans had already wiped out their own
natural forests and with them numerous plant and animal
species. Today, the northern part of continental Europe, and
most particularly northern France, Belgium, the Netherlands
and north-western Germany, looks more like one gigantic ego-
system than part of a living planet. Magmas of towns spread
out over the land, vast assemblages of factories, tangled

networks of roads and railways, interminable corridors of pipelines, mazes of shipping canals, and bundles of electricity cables, together constitute such a dense trellis that there is no longer any room for nature. The wild rabbits still existing have come to consider airports as the safest place to perpetuate their species, despite the battues that are organized to chase them away. This is the case at Charles de Gaulle airport, just north of Paris.

We, the privileged people, who have so ruthlessly taken advantage of all that industrialization has offered to us, have reached the limit of our exploitation of earth. We destroy, devour, and deplete everything in our path. We impose few restraints on ourselves. We develop to excess. On this planet, we have come to embody excess itself.

We have reached such a state of crisis that we have very possibly already passed the point of no return. As James Lovelock[iii] writes in *The Revenge of Gaia*, "The few things we know about the response of the Earth to our presence are deeply disturbing. Even if we stopped immediately all further seizing of Gaia's land and water for food and fuel production and stopped poisoning the air, it would take more than a thousand years to recover from the damage we have already done ..."[14]

Will nature help us to return to the sobriety of self-restraint?

[iii] James Lovelock is an independent English atmospheric scientist. He is the inventor of the electron capture detector that detects man-made chemicals. His detector was used to determine that pesticide residues were present in virtually all species on Earth and even in mothers' milk. He also used this type of detector to discover the man-made chlorofluorocarbons (CFCs) that are depleting the stratospheric ozone layer. James Lovelock is best known as author of the "Gaia hypothesis" named after the Greek goddess of the Earth.

CHAPTER 8

Beyond Consumerism

> *Executives who choose social and environmental goals over profit – who try to act morally – are, in fact, immoral ...*
> *Corporate social responsibility is thus illegal – at least when it is genuine.*
>
> *Joel Bakan* [15]

C onsumerism has changed the goals of industry. There was a time when the main function of industry was to produce goods to satisfy the needs of society. Of course, in order to sustain itself and remain competitive, it was always crucial for it to make a profit; any kind of business that is not profitable cannot survive very long. Today, industry has gone far beyond making a normal profit. The primary objective of many corporations is no longer to produce goods; it is now to produce money. Money used to be a means of exchange; now it is the product itself. Economism has replaced basic economics. Society has fallen into an unrestricted money culture.

American society is presently organized mostly according to the principle of economism which is actually to have no principles at all when it comes to making money. Money has to govern people's lives and their way of thinking. And it does. Individual behavior, traditional values, social affairs and politics are all subordinated to money. Culture and morality are expunged by the principles of economism. Those who criticize the way in which society is engineered to encourage consumerism in spite of itself, those who criticize the transformation of human enterprise into man-power enterprise where employees are interchangeable, are accused of being atavistic or of impeding Progress. As John Attarian stipulates, "Non-economic values, concerns, and aspects of life, such as national sovereignty, autonomy, identity, and cultural continuity ... are deemed chimerical .... Economism eventually turns everything into a commodity to be marketed at a profit."[16]

A first example showing the extent to which economism has penetrated American society concerns manufacturing. Many well-known American companies no longer produce any of the equipment or goods that established their reputation. They have transferred production to South East Asia and act now as simple warehouses for their products. Their only objective is money. It matters little to them if, in a matter of hours, thousands of skilled American workers who had served them for many years lost their jobs and their employee benefits, including health insurance. Or that the Asian factories that now manufacture their products offer miserable working conditions and nearly no social benefit to their employees.

A second example shows how credit cards have allowed economism to invade almost every business, from the smallest shops to supermarkets, doctors' offices and hospitals, leisure activities... Today, most prices include the fee that Visa, MasterCard and other credit companies charge to businesses. Everybody, be they card holders or those too poor to qualify for one, help pay the fees. But the poor, who pay cash, will never be able to take advantage of the credit or the enticement of free air mileage that the credit companies offer on each dollar spent. They can only watch the planes go by overhead. Credit card companies and banks have joined forces. Together they have invented a subtle "flying tax" that is imposed on all consumers.

The perverse effects of money have been known since coins were introduced and nearly every community in the world has struggled to devise ways, with more or less success, to counter them. The United States, allows free rein to the culture of money.

Economism acts like a dark screen obscuring the consequences of the decisions made by the consumer society. We do not see that we are exploiting workers in the Third World, that we are depleting the earth's most valuable resources and that we are destroying the balance of nature in all that we buy.

The money culture condemns our future. Economism will not prevail, but what will we substitute for it? Free enterprise and deregulation as a whole do not allow us to challenge our economic laws; in the USA, any deviation from the straight and narrow of current capitalism is considered subversive. The social-democratic system in Europe has shown that it is no better at sating the insatiability of the society on which it depends. A more socialistic approach would certainly be able to curb the excess of Development but it would still need to satisfy society's appetite.

Every social system developed by industrialized societies since Newcomen made his first steam engine breathe fire, from communism to capitalism, leads to the squandering of the earth's valuable resources and the destruction of our habitat.

CHAPTER 9

Democracy Made in Washington

Hostem populationibus prohibere.[i]

Julius Cæsar, ca 58 BC[17]

T he Second World War was different from all previous
wars. For the first time in human history, military war
machines were more important than infantrymen. It was the
first war to be so dependent on industry. To overcome the
powerful German and Japanese forces, the federal government
in Washington asked American industry to make an unprece-
dented effort to produce ever more powerful and efficient
boats, planes, tanks and all other sorts of weapons. In its
response, American industry was so efficient that by the end of
the war, its corporations had developed a manufacturing capa-
bility that considerably exceeded the actual needs of the North
American continent. In order to sustain themselves, they thus
needed to set up a commercial system extending far beyond
American borders.

The imperialist madness of the Germans, Italians and
Japanese had indirectly forced American industry to begin to
develop what would become the biggest industrial empire that

---

[i] "Prevent the enemy from rapine"

has ever existed. And the most formidable military arsenal in the process.

Paradoxically, at the end of the war, for all its industrial power the United States was unable to penetrate the markets of a great many countries that were still under colonial control. The Europeans had colonized virtually everything that was fit for colonization on earth and the relationships between the European countries and their colonies were very exclusive. England managed her colonies in such a way that they only had relationships with her, just as she had done with her colonies in North America before the United States gained independence. France, Belgium, Spain, and Portugal did the same with their colonies. To clearly mark their possessions, the European countries had enclosed their colonies behind well defined, but often artificial, boundaries. This was the case in the Middle East and most of the African continent. In each of these newly defined territories, an administration had been put in place based on the governing principles of the colonizing country. The laws applied in Mozambique were copied from those of Portugal; Kenyan laws greatly resembled those of England; and the laws of the Belgian Congo were Belgian.

This situation obviously did not please the incumbents of the White House and one can imagine them digging through the archives to find the procedures that had allowed President Theodore Roosevelt to put in place his "open door" policy in China at the very end of the 19th century.

Colonization had given to the countries of the Middle East and Africa clear geographical boundaries and governments that had well established laws and procedures. Now, they only needed to gain independence in order to become fully fledged nations. After often very bloody wars, and in many cases with the discreet support of the United States, one after another they began to gain the right to actually exist as independent nations. By 1970, practically all of the countries in those regions that had been colonized by Western Europe had freed themselves, with the exception of a few islands that had chosen to remain attached to their "mother" countries.

In reality, the countries that had been newly promoted to the status of nations still had not gained real independence. While they could claim to govern themselves, be protected by the Charter of Nations and sit on most of the UN and other prestigious international organizations, they were not really economically independent. Generally underdeveloped industrially and poorly trained in international economic policy, either because of cultural differences or a lack of know-how, they remained easy prey for the industrialized nations. Even today, most of them are still economically subject to the "developed" countries.

In the new game of world domination, ego-systems, rather than nations themselves as was the case in the colonialist era, now prey on the weaker nations. The process of ego-systemization has replaced that of colonization. Colonization assumed that the colonizing country would involve itself in the colony's government, including education and social services. Ego-systems are not concerned with such delicate matters. They cut straight to the goal that interests them. This principle does not, however, prevent predator-countries from imposing their ego-systems by force should it prove necessary to do so. In these circumstances, the forcefulness of any such intervention really depends on just how badly the predator-country's ego-systems want to prey on the resources in question.

The process of ego-systemization demands the subjection of the "yet-to-be developed" prey-country to the economic will of the "developed" predator-country. There are many strategies that may be applied to achieve this. On this point it seems that there are no limits to the imagination.

The ego-systemization of a country can take place through "friendly" diplomatic channels. In the 1930s, the King of Saudi Arabia, Abd-el-Aziz III Ibn Saud, having unified his country, considered himself to be a great monarch but he lacked the means of supporting a lifestyle befitting his status. His palace was just made of local clay and his meager harem was woefully inadequate for a man of his station. He began to tire of seeing his kingdom completely overlooked by geologists who were scouring the Middle East prospecting for major oil fields. In 1933, after many years of haggling and finally negotiating, the King was glad to grant oil and gas exploration rights to Standard Oil of California. Twelve years later, this company merged with three other major American oil companies to form Aramco, which had an exclusive oil prospecting concession covering practically the whole of Saudi Arabia, and now it was able to distribute Saudi crude oil around the world.

Between 1945 and the nationalization of Saudi oil in 1976, the kingdom of the Wahhabis was dependent on the major American corporations to carry out the developments that were recommended by its advisers – who were also American. With the royalties that Aramco paid to the king, the palaces of Riyadh grew inordinately vast; majestic airports popped up from the sand; new towns, fully air-conditioned, appeared as if by magic. Whether these developments were superfluous, like the palaces, or more utilitarian, like the country infrastructure, they were carried out mainly by American corporations. In the end, most of the money theoretically made by Saudi Arabia went straight to the USA. Aramco was a cornucopia for the American economy.

Until 1976, the other oligarchies of the Arabian Peninsula, namely Kuwait, the United Arab Emirates, Qatar, and Oman, also functioned primarily for the benefit of the United States. Even if after that date, companies from various countries in Europe and Asia, as well as the US, built industrial facilities throughout the entire Arabian Peninsula, the principle has not really changed. The Gulf States remain subject to the ego-systems of industrialized nations to whom they sell their precious oil.

The ego-systemization of a country can also be speeded up considerably by the corruption of a few unscrupulous senior "dignitaries" who, for money, will happily sell their countries' resources to foreign predators. The petroleum ego-systems set up in Nigeria, for example, sustain the apparently limitless corruption of that country's leaders. The Nigerian people living near the oil wells gain no benefit from the manna drawn from the ground, only a few yards away from their huts. All they get is the pollution generated in the oil fields. The Western oil operators do not hear their grievances; they only care about their official contracts.

The "virus" of corruption is as old as the world. It is all the easier for predatory companies to practice, given that it is very often already the norm in their own countries. In the city of Washington DC alone, the capital of the United States, "some 14,000 registered lobbyists influence the legislation and policies put forth by Congress, the White House and more than 200 federal agencies."[18] Among the most effective means of persuasion for lobbyists are those that take into account the personal interests of the politicians. These corrupting intermediaries are just as present in Paris, Rome, London and other European capitals as they are in Washington but, unlike what is more or less the rule in the United States, lobbyists in Europe are not generally listed as such on the registers of commerce. The corruptors, whether they are 110-meter hurdle runners, cabaret singers, retired admirals, blonde bombshells, or side-lined politicians, all discreetly try to subject their prey to the ego-systems for which they "work."

Contrary to what is generally reported in the main Western press, lobbying was more difficult to organize in Baghdad under Saddam Hussein than it has traditionally been in Paris or Washington. Under Hussein, any person caught favoring a visiting predator was imprisoned. A number of members of the Iraqi government were, after a hasty "trial," removed to some unofficial prison, sometimes disappearing forever, for this offence.

The methods of subjecting a country to a foreign ego-system can be very elaborate. One of these methods consists of making it clear to the prey-country that if it wishes to achieve the privileged status of a "developing" nation, or even a "developed" nation, it will need to set up a modernization plan for its key sectors. In *Confessions of an Economic Hit Man*, John Perkins describes the many tactics, some of which he tried out himself, that can be used to achieve this end: "My job ... was to encourage world leaders to become part of a vast network that promotes US commercial interests. In the end, those leaders become ensnared in a web of debt that ensures their loyalty. We can draw on them whenever we desire – to satisfy our political, economic, or military needs. In turn, they bolster their political positions by bringing industrial parks, power plants, and airports to their people. The owners of [concerned] US engineering/construction companies become fabulously wealthy."[19]

If the "soft" tactics have ultimately failed but a country's resources are still considered essential to the predator-country, the latter will attempt to open the doors by more persuasive action. This might take the form of aid given discretely to organize a coup d'état in the hope of replacing the current government with a government favorable *de facto* to the predator.

Iran experienced this type of enforced submission in the 1950s. Dr. Mossadeq was elected Prime Minister by the Iranian parliament in 1951. He promptly overthrew the Shah and created a national oil committee to examine the nationalization of the country's oil resources and assets. When Mossadeq acted on its recommendation to nationalize them, it was the first time that an oil country had nationalized the whole of its hydrocarbon production infrastructure that had been set up by foreign companies on its soil. This was a huge turning point in the history of oil, and in Iranian history too. But it was not a real victory for Dr. Mossadeq; Europe and the United States, who were presented with this *fait accompli*, were confident of being able to obtain sufficient quantities of hydrocarbons from other exporting countries so, in 1952, they imposed a total embargo on Iranian oil. This made things very difficult economically for Dr. Mossadeq who discovered at the same time that his position was threatened internally by actions orchestrated in Iran by the British and US governments. In 1953, "Leaflets describing Mossadeq as a Communist collaborator flooded Tehran. A huge demonstration was organized, ostensibly of pro-Shah sympathizers but in fact of hired thugs."[20]

Mossadeq had no choice but to give in. On August 19, Radio Tehran announced that General Zahedi had been appointed prime minister and that Mossadeq had fled. The Americans had done what was needed for the Shah to resume the absolute monarchy of Iran. This time, however, the Shah would know that he needed to keep his gaze fixed on the West.

All that remained to do to keep Iran in the service of the West was to reinforce the Shah's power. One of Washington's main concerns was to reorganize the Iranian army, the army being the best guarantee for maintaining a regime. While an emperor may let his people believe that he is the worthy representative of a dynasty, his imperial seat is nonetheless better secured if he also surrounds himself with a solid praetorian guard. The Iranian generals were chosen from amongst the most faithful to the Shah and the Iranian army was soon transformed into a force far greater than warranted. It was modernized and equipped almost entirely with such sophisticated American equipment that it required the assistance of thousands of military advisers, who were also American. Not only was the political system of the Shah thus ensured for the next 25 years, but the United States had also succeeded in establishing in Iran a formidable military ego-system that required an unending supply of equipment "made in the USA." By 1969, the Iranian sovereign even felt secure enough to crown himself the Shahinshah – "King of Kings" – at Persepolis, the ancient capital of the Persian Empire. His Imperial Majesty Mohammed Reza Pahlavi ruled Iran as an absolute monarch. Relying on his powerful army and a secret police among the most ruthless in the world, he ruled the country with an iron hand and brooked no opposition. Unfounded denunciation was common practice and opponents of the regime were readily placed behind bars. The prisons were full, the interrogations were summary, and the return home was rare.

With a monarch favorable to Western style Development, Iran became an ideal place for international business. The opening of Iran to the West was facilitated by the complicity of the rich Iranian families. Eager to profit outrageously from Iran's Development, they were willing to involve their country in a widespread swindle. On nationalist pretexts, it was made extremely difficult for foreign companies to obtain construction contracts in Iran without the "help" of intermediaries who all claimed to have connections to the highest authorities in the realm. Such "help" proved to be very costly. The importing of materials and equipment was also subject to bribery systems. Companies that had signed contracts with Iran to carry out industrial projects in the country had to buy their cement – tens of thousands of tons – at prices six or seven times the official price fixed by the royal authorities. This hidden "extra" cost applied to cement imported from Europe, as well as to cement bought in Iran where most of the cement factories belonged to the royal family. "Special taxes" could be levied overnight on any type of imported material.

The rich Iranians who were in charge of their country's Development had every interest to contract with foreign companies for the construction of Iran's oil infrastructure, power stations, dams and industrial plants in general, rather than with Iranian companies that would not be able to guarantee the same shady benefits. Iran was plundered for the benefit of the rich Iranian families; from 1970 to 1978, forty per cent or more of the overall internal revenue of the country was thus transferred to private foreign bank accounts. Development of the country's social infrastructure offered few opportunities for the quick and reliable enrichment of the moneyed class; therefore it was neglected. In 1978, Tehran, a city of more than ten million inhabitants, still did not have a sewage network, even in the most luxurious area of the city where the Shah and the super-rich families lived. When there were storms, torrents of water would gush down the wide avenues located at the base of the Alborz Mountains to the lower parts of the city where the poor people lived.

Of course, the foreign ego-systems "attached" to Iran had no desire for change. But in 1978, under pressure from humanitarian organizations, some foreign governments decided nonetheless that the Iranian regime had reached a peak in terms of tyranny, and they no longer wished to support it. The American and French presidents, Jimmy Carter and Valéry Giscard d'Estaing, were amongst them. Without full support of the West, the Shah was unable to prevent the Islamic Revolution that gave control of the country to Ayatollah Khomeini. The process of ego-systemization of Iran by foreign countries was interrupted.

When a predator-country is unable to subjugate by "traditional" means a country whose resources it covets, it may consider military action as the surest way for securing its prey. The model of this type of intervention is the invasion of Iraq by the US-UK coalition in March 2003.

This strong-armed intervention, which was only supposed to last for a few weeks, placed Iraq under the control of the United States. Very soon after the invasion, Washington installed in Baghdad a government led by a US administrator, in reality a "proconsul," who had total control of Iraq. Just after making this assignment, President G.W. Bush signed Executive Order 13303, granting American oil contractors involved in the Iraqi oil business "a lifetime exemption from lawsuits."[21]

I, George W. Bush, President of the United States of America, ... order:

Unless licensed or otherwise authorized pursuant to this order, any attachment, judgment, decree, lien, execution, garnishment, or other judicial process is prohibited, and shall be deemed null and void, with respect of the following:

(a) the Development Fund for Iraq, and

(b) all Iraqi petroleum and petroleum products and interests, ...proceeds, obligations, or any financial instruments ... [attached to them] that are in the United States, that hereafter come within the US, or that are or hereafter come within the possession or control of US persons.*

* The term 'United States persons' means any US citizen, permanent resident alien ... corporation, group, subgroup or other [US] organization.[22]

In early July 2003, the American proconsul appointed 25 members to form the Iraqi Governing Council, which was to govern the country, under his direct authority, for a provisional period. Amongst these "elected" were Iraqis, such as Ahmed Chalabi, who had been directly imported from the United States. At the beginning of 2004, the proconsul arranged for the 25 puppets of this Council to "democratically" approve the basic principles on which the future Iraqi constitution would be drawn up.

In 2008, after five years of occupation of the country, and after having – directly or indirectly – brought about the death of hundreds of thousands of innocent Iraqis, the United States still had not succeeded in setting up in Baghdad a government that will guarantee the ego-systemization of Iraq by American corporations. It has led the country into a bloody civil war that will require years to die down. Afraid of being tried for treason in their own country, the Iraqi political figures who have supported the American intervention still do not want the American army to leave Iraq. The American army is also unable to leave without the risk of bringing to light all the war crimes that were committed, and which, in the end, have served only to give international terrorists further reasons for attacking the West. Following its imperialist strategy, Washington DC is building fortresses for its soldiers in Iraq. It is positioning itself near its prey because it expects to continue to plunder it indefinitely. The war is certainly expensive for Americans but all the US money spent on Iraq does not really leave the United States. The majority of it simply goes from the pockets of American taxpayers to the bank accounts of the American corporations involved in the war, with a brief stint in the federal coffers in between. It is thus in the interest of the corporations serving the US military that the Iraqi civil war situation does not improve. It is also in the interest of their employees who have good jobs.

On the other hand, the American oil corporations that followed close behind their army to set up the tentacles of their ego-systems in Iraq, still cannot be sure of success. This is despite the fact that their proconsul who arrived in Baghdad in 2003 moved as fast as he could to help them. Just a few days after his arrival, he had already done what was necessary to ensure that the state-owned companies managing the country's essential resources were privatized to the benefit of "persons" favorable to setting up an "American democracy." The swindling of Iraq, legally organized, could now theoretically begin.

It seems that democracies not "made in Washington" are becoming less and less commendable. As has been the case since the year 2000, once the American leaders identify a prey-country, they generally hide their true intentions and announce the urgency of importing a good dose of "American democracy" into that country. It is as if they are talking about some "social substance" of which the United States has a surplus that it wanted to offload. As Edward Peck, former US Ambassador in Iraq in the 1970s put it: "This affirmation is nonsense for a start. By definition and etymologically, democracy cannot be imported by a country; it must be the fruit borne of the people themselves."[23]

In any event, the behavior of the United States contradicts its official line. When it comes to building predatory relations with another country, Washington above all likes to deal with governments who are not subject to re-election. The American government is then able to develop "very personal" economic strategies with potentates whose authority will not be called into question by their people a few months later. The kings and princes who currently rule the Arabian Peninsula are "reliable." They are by and large highly respected by the whole of the "developed" world. They profit so outrageously from their position as dynasts that the word corruption ceases to have any meaning when applied to them. Louis XIV was never treated as corrupt in his palace at Versailles. He was the Sun King by right.

CHAPTER 10

Imperial Ethic

We fired 'shake and bake' missions at the insurgents, using white phosphorous to flush them out and high explosives to take them out.

Lt. Col. Barry Venable[i]

With these words, Lieutenant Colonel Barry Venable, Pentagon spokesman, was alluding to the way in which the American troops led their attack on the Iraqi town of Fallujah in November 2004.

The American, French, Italian and other journalists who tried to approach Fallujah were either imprisoned, taken hostage or expelled. The "insurgents" in question were likely members of the Iraqi resistance who were trying to free their country from the US-UK coalition that had come to install their ego-systems. Those of greatest interest to the coalition were the oil and military corporations.

It would seem that "developed" nations have no ethic other than that which enables them to increase their industrial power.

In brandishing the standard of "democracy," the actions of the United States demonstrate that it believes itself authorized to impose its power on the rest of the world. The tentacles

---

[i] November 15, 2005.

of its ego-systems spread out relentlessly around the globe seizing anything that might be of economic interest. When it meets resistance in a prey-country, Washington declares that country to be dangerous to world security and the CIA is discreetly called in to take care of it. Then, if need be, the Pentagon is asked to intervene, again to protect "democracy." For thirty years, at one time or another, the Philippines, El Salvador, Cuba, Libya, Chile, Guatemala, Panama, Iran, Colombia, Iraq and most recently Venezuela, amongst others, were declared threats because their leaders were either dictators, communists, Nazis, drug-traffickers or corrupt or possessed madmen. This is how the United States portrays those who try to disengage themselves from the imperialistic ego-systems it is imposing on them. Most of these countries underwent, and in some cases are still undergoing, "democratic-style" military interventions. In almost every case, they were "invited" to install governments that would accommodate American practices.

The US corporations that were forced to leave Cuba in 1959 when Castro seized power have still not managed to return to the island. The country is declared to be under a dangerous communist dictatorship despite the fact that its military capabilities are extremely modest. China, on the other hand, where Western corporations have the luxury of unlimited exploitation of its enormous labor force, is not considered to be a threat even though it keeps a fifth of the world's population under the red communist flag and possesses an impressive nuclear arsenal to secure its future ambitions.

So far, Islamic Iran has managed to avoid receiving a massive dose of "democracy" but the country has not been overlooked. Americans and Europeans, among others, censure it for wanting to produce uranium fuel on its own territory. The Europeans seem to be forgetting that they sought Iran's help to build a uranium enrichment plant on their own continent. In the early 1970s, His Imperial Majesty the Shah of Iran Mohammed Reza Pahlavi was invited to take a 10% share in a new company Eurodif, the *Société Européenne d'Enrichissement d'Uranium par Diffusion Gazeuse*. The plant was built in the southern France a few years later. Along with France, Spain and Belgium, Iran still holds a 10% share in Eurodif, which supplies nuclear fuel to around forty electric energy producers worldwide.

The European uranium enrichment plant was not the only nuclear project in which Iran was involved in the 1970s. Germany and France each sold Iran a nuclear electrical power plant to be constructed in the province of Khuzestan. To comply with the international rules Iran had to create the Iranian Atomic Energy Organization. Many Iranian engineers were also sent to foreign universities for training so that they would be able to take charge of the new nuclear facilities. Since then, these engineers have continued to carry out the work that the Europeans invited them to undertake. Construction of the two nuclear power stations was interrupted in 1979 when Ayatollah Khomeini seized power, but in 1994, Iran granted the completion of one of these projects to the Russians.

Given that both Iran's oil and natural gas reserves are the second largest in the world, it is testament to the talents of the German and French diplomats that they persuaded the Shah to invest in nuclear energy in his own country. The nuclear project that the Europeans undertook in the name of Progress is still on track and no one in Iran seems prepared to question its course. Why should Progress be stopped specifically in their country?

Is the West's position against the Iranian uranium enrichment program directed by a peace promoting ethic? If so, the Iranians might take umbrage today at receiving peace lessons from countries that go to war as easily as they go to the oil market, particularly given the fact that the last time Iran directly attacked another was more than 1,400 years ago, in 602 AD, when Khosrow II, King of Persia, launched the last great Persian invasion of the Byzantine Empire.

Michael Parenti, in his book *Against Empire*, is certainly right in saying that the American secret service spends a great deal of time inventing enemies:

US leaders must convince the American people that the immense costs of empire are necessary for their security and survival. For years we were told that the great danger we faced was 'the World Communist Menace with its headquarters in Moscow.' Since the demise of the USSR, our political leaders have been warning us that the world is full of other dangerous adversaries, who, apparently had been previously overlooked. ... This scenario of a world of enemies was used by the rulers of the Roman Empire and by nineteenth-century British imperialists. Enemies always had to be confronted, requiring more interventions and more expansion. And if enemies were not to be found, they were invented.[24]

As early as 1976, Earl Cook was asking questions about the ethic behind the attitudes and conduct of industrialized countries:

Under what conditions, if any, can a nation justify taking for its own use the nonrenewable resources of other nations too weak economically or military to use or protect those resources?[25]

American ego-systems do not always spread their tentacles directly from the United States. Sometimes they do so from bases established in neutral countries. This enables them to keep certain operations anonymous. The Arabian Peninsula is particularly well-suited for this type of deployment. It has the advantage of offering great economic and political security and it is well protected by the US military. In the event of a serious financial crisis, the Arabian Peninsula's banks of black gold will be more reliable than traditional banks. Anonymous corporations can be set up there to intervene discreetly in the whole world, including the United States or Europe. In 2006, one of them, Dubai Ports World, with strong support from the White House, tried to get a financial interest in the company managing many American ports, including New York, Baltimore, New Orleans, Miami and Philadelphia. On the grounds of security, the American Congress did however manage to oppose this subtle maneuver.

American ego-systems are not the only ones seeking to conquer natural or human resources worldwide. The Europeans, the Japanese and the Chinese also do everything in their power to subject "undeveloped countries" to industrial law. France "assists" a number of African countries. In 2006, British Prime Minister Tony Blair announced with much political fanfare what he called a "Marshall Plan" in Africa, but China was already discretely there.

The ego-systems of "developed" countries plague the world. An initial gift of money to a least "developed" country can start up a system of industrial exploitation in favor of the initiator. This is a classic way of making poor countries dependent on industrialized countries. The process is admirably described by John Perkins in *Confessions of an Economic Hit Man.*[26] In the guise of globalization, rich countries force poor countries to adopt industrial developments that very often conform neither to their culture nor their interests. These countries are treated with the same carelessness as were the gold and silver mines of Nevada. For "developed" countries they are, in fact, just "mines." Once the desired resource is exhausted or no longer profitable, the ego-system will withdraw from the country and leave behind the waste products of its intervention. It also will abandon the population that served it during its operations. Michael Parenti, in *Against Empire,* has his own interpretation of globalization: "Designed to leave the world's economic destiny to the tender mercy of bankers and multinational corporations, globalization is a logical extension of imperialism, a victory of empire over republic, international finance over democracy."[27]

All the above is an everyday reality, but what are we, the "educated," the "intellectuals," the "developed" ones, doing to curb the course of ego-systemization of countries where it is not wanted? What is our ethic towards countries whose resources are being plundered for our benefit?

Many of us send our children to schools that will guarantee them a place in the society of Progress. They will find work as lawyers, researchers, engineers, technicians, architects, financiers, insurers, advertising agents, salesmen and military officers. Many will participate – directly or indirectly – in the development of invading ego-systems. They will act "honestly," as I believed I was doing for so many years. They will have faith in what they are doing. Why? Never ask why. They might be forced to lie to themselves. We might also believe them.

What is our ethic?

Part II

Science Dogmas

CHAPTER 11

You Don't Stop Progress!

When I look at society around me, I sometimes feel as if I am in a dream. I find it hard to believe that we are serious when we claim to be following the path of Progress because, in reality, all together we are acting as if we want to ravage our planet.

It also seems to me that we are not really masters of our behavior. Looking back at my youth, I feel that it was society rather than myself that led me to become an engineer and then a "developer."

Recently, as I was meditating on the dilemma that exists between the individual and society, a strange notion came to my mind. I imagined a young graduate who, straight out of university, and prodded along by society, suddenly found himself on a moving train. He was in a compartment full of very busy looking people. Some of them were discussing industrial projects, others were writing reports, and others were confidently drawing endless diagrams on large sheets of paper. All of them looked very serious and were dressed in suits. It was clear that they were the same sort of people and that they were all old hands on this journey.

Realizing the strangeness of the situation, the young man ventured to ask the least unapproachable passenger, "Excuse me, sir, could you tell me where this train is headed?"

Astonished to hear such a surprising question, the other snapped back, "It is going to Progress! You are on the Train of Progress!"

Confused by this reply, the young intruder braved a second question, "Do you know what the next stop is?"

At this the other became angry and shouted in reply, "Didn't anyone tell you, it doesn't stop? You don't stop Progress!"

The new passenger, feeling increasingly uncomfortable, reluctantly summoned the courage to ask a third question, "Do you think I might be able to talk to the conductor...?"

By now completely exasperated, the other passenger did not even allow the young man to finish his question before he exploded, "There is no conductor and there is no engineer either! You would do better to just get down to work like the rest of us here."

Afraid of arousing general indignation, the young man decided to be quiet. He looked at the various compartments and finally settled in the one that seemed to be the least inhospitable. Then, as he had been advised to do, he got down to work – taking up the same activity as the others.

Within a few weeks, he had become a full fledged passenger of the Train hurtling towards Progress. Within a few years, he was even one of its most active members.

That young man's experience seems strikingly similar to my own and to that of many of us who have taken the Train of Progress and have helped speed it along, and possibly have even added new coaches to it. But I fear that, once we board the Train, we no longer have the opportunity or even the curiosity to broach the questions that were posed by that young newcomer.

Today, I find it amazing that I never felt the need to curb my enthusiasm over the years that I spent on the Train. I find it equally amazing that I never met anyone who ever really dared to imagine slowing down the relentless machine. Was the passenger who told the young man, "You don't stop Progress!" right? Once we are on board, do we become blind to everything that happens in its wake? Can we no longer think freely? Is the solidarity that we develop with each other over time just a means to continually increase the speed of the Train, regardless of the cost to the future of humanity?

Finally, are there any emergency brakes on the Train?

This disturbing question concerns all industrialized societies. Without claiming to have the answer, I thought it opportune to turn the question first on myself and no longer hide behind the impersonal concept that I call "industrial society." I needed to know how I had allowed myself to be so carried away by the Train of Progress; how I had managed to block out acknowledgement of the developmental excess to which I had been a party. So, I mentally retraced my steps. I envisaged myself back at school. Then I thought of the places where I had, so very conscientiously, helped to build industrial plants that form part of the world's most invasive ego-systems; and I tried to understand how I had become such a devotee of industrial development, so blind to life.

CHAPTER 12

Devoutly Yours

During my university training, I never noticed the ephemeral nature of our industrial development. I never understood that it was just a passing stage in Western society or that there was every reason to mistrust it, as much for its over-zealousness and its excess as for its brevity. How could I have been so blind, from the very beginning of my professional life, to something so elemental to our future? What made me board the Train of Progress?

My maternal grandparents were farmers on the harsh mountain plateaus of the Massif Central in France. They met the majority of their needs by producing their own cereals, vegetables, poultry, dairy products and livestock; they lived almost self-sufficiently. No motor ever entered their farm. After nightfall, a feeble electric lamp hanging from the ceiling would cast mysterious areas of shadow around the main room whose floor was hewn from the very granite on which the farm was built. Candlesticks accompanied them to bed. The rest of the house was left to darkness, and to the cats and mice.

The whole village lived according to the rhythm of the sun. Days of toil followed days of toil. The cycle of work corresponded to the cycle of the seasons. The years brought few changes in activities. Everything was traditional. One day I asked my uncle why he was growing his wheat in several small plots instead of grouping them together as one. In fact, he did the same with all his other main crops. It seemed to me that it would have been more efficient to group them together, but he explained to me that in the mountains it was unwise to do so because the fields were never subjected to the same conditions of spring frosts, rain, hail, summer droughts or insect attacks. Dividing up the crops helped minimize the risks. My question showed that school had already steered me towards blind Development.

In my notion of efficiency, there was no place for frosts, droughts, hailstones or insects. Moreover, I had failed to take into account the fact that, without agricultural machinery, my uncle could not grow and harvest more than his simple means allowed. He had a duty to be prudent.

Curbs on change, and more particularly on excessive agricultural development, certainly existed in those traditional little mountain farms. It was not there that I would find the source of my propensity for change. The Train of Progress did not pass through the plateaus of the Massif Central. I needed to look elsewhere, further away.

At the base of the plateau there was an industrial valley that had been developed at the end of the eighteen century. In those days, factories were fueled by coal so they were located near the coal mines and also on rivers that could carry away their waste products. As this valley met these criteria, mines, steelworks and metallurgical industries were united there for better or worse. It was in one of these valley towns that my parents settled.

If you grow up in an industrial town in which the drop hammers strike day and night in nearby steelworks, a career in industry seems to make perfect sense. It is certainly why, one day in October 1952, I set aside the philosophy classes that I had so loved, burned the hundreds of poems that I had written to alleviate the tedium of some of my other classes, and without great enthusiasm, submitted myself to the rigors of obtaining an engineering degree. My acceptance at an engineering school was the first step to boarding the Train of Progress. At the time, however, I was obviously very far from seeing the significance of my entrance to that school.

The school that had accepted me had the unusual feature of being set inside the ancient Abbey of Cluny located in southern Burgundy. All that remained of the Abbey was the cloister and the ruins of the Romanesque church surrounded by a large garden. The monks had abandoned the monastery during the years following the strongly anticlerical French Revolution of 1789 and the Romanesque church was then sold to builders who used it as a quarry for building stones. After Napoleon became emperor in 1801, he allowed the quarrying to continue until the church was almost completely destroyed. The only parts left standing are the southern transept and one of its four bell towers.

The state established the school in the cloister that adjoined the remnants of the Abbey church. The day that I arrived there it was raining as it often can in that region at that time of year and the stone walls reeked of damp. The window panes seemed very small and the high ceilings struck me as being well-suited for monastic meditation. When I entered the courtyard of the cloister, I felt as if I had gone back in time to medieval days when the study of science was considered to be a dangerous practice for the mind. The objectives of the school and those of the medieval monastery seemed so fundamentally antithetical to me that I could not understand how engineers could get an education in a place so symbolic of so spiritual a past.

In the weeks that followed, the professors soon made me forget the spiritual aspect of the place, as did the eagerness of the upper-classmates to integrate us into the extra curricular activities. I no longer had any free time to dwell on the dampness of the old stones or the ceiling heights. Like many others before me, I became a student engineer. During my three years there we were taught all that could be of use to future industrialists.

On the other hand, nothing in the teaching and nothing in our everyday life ever referred to the glorious history of the

Abbey of Cluny during the Middle Ages. Of course there were always plenty of tourists who came eager to learn its history but the abbey guarded its secrets about its past. The tour guides were forthcoming about Cluny's importance in the European monastic world of the Middle Ages, but they said little about the Abbey's intellectual leadership during the height of its power. It was as if the subjects were incongruous.

It was purely by chance that the Abbey came to house this modern school, which could just as easily have been situated in other buildings less charged with history. So there was no reason to include the Abbey's history in our curriculum. Nevertheless, the walls were there and I felt their silence. They seemed to have so much to say; and our lessons paid so little heed to what they knew. Their silence made me feel slightly uneasy when I was inside. It is possible that some of the teachers felt the same but they could not go against their educational duty by acknowledging it to us. Their task was to prepare us to take the Train of Progress without a backward thought.

The thinkers who had led Europe into the Enlightenment, and into the French Revolution of 1789 and the harsh political regimes that followed, had long convinced the French people of the need to make a complete break with a past, which was seen as "medieval" and inappropriate for the Development of society. Science, economics, and technology were the tools of the future. It mattered little that the Second World War, still so recent, had revealed the dangers of technology. It mattered little that to support the future it was necessary to sail across several seas to bring back rubber, minerals and other substances from continents around the globe. It mattered little that France was already beginning to run out of energy resources on its own soil. On the contrary, these dangers, or constraints, were seen as reasons for preparing the country to overcome them. The future would be defined by science and technology. Engineering diplomas invited those holding them to pursue Development. A school for engineers was not going to encourage one to stop and analyze the concerns of the past, even if it was set in the cloister of a medieval Abbey. Like many others, the school in Cluny taught the foundations on which to build the most effective, rational, scientific and economic future ego-systems. Period.

While I feel greatly indebted to it and its professors for the quality of teaching that I received there, I do regret that no course in the syllabus ever questioned the foundations and values of the type of Development that we were being trained to lead. Above all, I regret that there was never any reference made to all those who, in the past, had attached such importance to this fundamental subject; in particular, the ancient philosophers, the thinkers of the pre-industrial period, those who stayed at the Abbey during its monastic period and also their Muslim, Chinese and Indian counterparts. The great minds of the past had thought long and hard about the very questions that we, on the other hand, have just swept under the carpet in our rush for Progress. Their meditations might have enlightened us, but we were not there to meditate.

The Abbey of Cluny was founded in 912 in accordance with the rule of St Benedict by William the Pious, Duke of Aquitaine, who was anxious to protect his soul and that of his wife Engelberge and other loved ones, " 'Because I wish to provide for my salvation whilst there is still time, [...] I have deemed it [...] necessary to set aside for the benefit of my soul a small portion of the worldly goods which have been bestowed on me. [...] May prayers, requests and supplications constantly be addressed [in the future Abbey of Cluny] to the Lord as much for me as for my [wife ...].' "[8] The Abbey reached the height of its importance under the Abbot Peter the Venerable. From 1122 to 1156, it held sway over more than 1,000 priories spread out over a vast community that extended from the kingdoms of Portugal, Leon and Castile to the Kingdom of Scotland including the kingdoms of France, England, Wales, and the Holy Roman Empire. At the time Cluny was the seat of the largest medieval monastic order in the West. "The Abbot of Cluny acted as a mediator between the political powers and the papacy."[9] Fittingly, the Abbey's

Romanesque church was also the most impressive church in all of Europe, with its 470 foot long nave, two transepts and four bell-towers.

In medieval Europe, education was strictly controlled by the Roman Church and consisted of the seven liberal arts: grammar, dialectics, rhetoric, arithmetic, geometry, music and astronomy. These arts, which were taught in Latin, might seem rudimentary today. Grammar was basically the art of writing. Dialectics was that of organizing sentences. Rhetoric consisted of constructing arguments around an idea. Arithmetic taught mostly numbers and their fractions. Geometry was the study of space and volumes based on the works of Euclid. Astronomy essentially involved the study of the influence of the celestial bodies on the earth, and music sought to express that celestial harmony.

The European monastic schools played an important role in higher education but authorities also granted to certain eminent theologians the right to set up their own schools, some of which attained considerable intellectual significance. The school of Peter Abelard[i] on Mount Sainte-Geneviève in Paris was one of these; he taught theology and philosophy and his school was known throughout Europe. Abelard was not, however, a model teacher of Christianity. He displayed a freedom of thought that led his friend, Peter the Venerable, Abbot of Cluny, to call him "the Socrates of France, the sublime Plato of the West, our Aristotle."[ii] His principle of "believing only that which can be explained" led to his being considered a "dangerous soul" by other eminent theologians such as Bernard of Clairvaux[iii] who, alluding to Abelard, wrote to the

---

[i] Peter Abelard, 1079-1142, was a pre-eminent philosopher and theologian of the 12th century. His luckless affair with Heloise made him a tragic figure of romance and his conflict with Bernard of Clairvaux over reason and religion made him a hero of the Enlightenment.

[ii] Epitaph to Abelard in the Père-Lachaise cemetery in Paris where Abelard and his wife Heloise are buried together.

[iii] Bernard of Clairvaux, 1090-1153, principal *maître à penser* (literally "master for thinking" or teacher of a way of thinking) of the Cistercian order which had 350 monasteries in Europe at the time of his death.

Pope, "What is more contrary to reason than trying to use reason to go beyond reason? What is more contrary to faith than refusing to believe anything which reason cannot grasp?"[30] When, in 1140, Abelard was finally excommunicated by Rome, he found refuge in the community of Cluny through his friend Peter the Venerable.

Despite the considerable audience that Abelard had in the Middle Ages, he never troubled our lessons at Cluny when I was there. Had he been invited to teach, he could have spoken to us about the difficulties that he had faced to exercise his talents. He could have shown us that the use of reason alone does not always solve all problems. Had we studied Abelard's thoughts, we would have learned that at one time society put powerful brakes on Progress. Maybe the Church was not wholly responsible for those restrictions, as we are often inclined to think today. Maybe the people of the Middle Ages intuitively knew that it would be better not to place complete trust in human enterprise. While this period is distant from us now, it would have been instructive to broach this subject, if only to arouse our curiosity.

When I left Cluny, I knew nothing about Abelard other than the old story passed down by students, which was that the product of his emasculation[iv] was buried under the enormous old oak tree bearing his name that towered majestically in the Abbey park. This was truly a minimum of information to learn about such a unique individual who so profoundly shook up European thinking at the time. In any event, it was part of the student lore at Cluny.

At the time of Abelard, the West was not totally impervious to the scientific approach. At the Muslim University of Cordova, in Andalusia, the finest scholars had been teaching

---

[iv] Canon Fulbert asked Peter Abelard to complete the education of his niece Heloise. Some time later, Heloise gave birth to a son she named Peter Astrolabe. Heloise at first refused to marry her lover Abelard so as not to sully his reputation. Their marriage did nonetheless probably take place. Canon Fulbert took revenge on Abelard by subjecting him to the dreadful punishment of castration.

the art, philosophy and science of Ancient Greeks for a long time. Cordova's "glory was the great library established by the Caliph Al Hakam II … who ruled from 961 to 976. Founding it 'Al Hakam made Cordova shine like a lighthouse upon the darkness of Europe.' … [It was] the greatest library the world had ever seen. Ultimately it contained 400,000 volumes …"[31] The library at the Abbey of Cluny seems to have contained at most 570 volumes. While the volumes were primarily written by members of the clergy, there were also some Aristotle, Cicero and Boethius to be read.[32]

The great Moorish sages of the University of Cordova dealt freely with scientific questions without feeling that they were necessarily calling into question the basic tenets of the Koran. "Al-Hallaj, more of a mystic than a scientist, taught that Allah continuously and endlessly creates and recreates atoms, arranging them according to his pleasure to form transient bodies of fleeting existence. Only the atom exists, was and always will be. The universe, a human being, a crystal are nothing but atoms assembled and disassembled as God wills."[33]

During the centuries that the Muslim school taught science, philosophy, medicine and methods of agricultural development at the gates to Europe, Andalusian society did not let itself get carried away by unrestrained Development. But Catholic Spain never accepted the principles of Muslim society. Finally, in 1492, the united armies of King Ferdinand of Aragon and Queen Isabella of Castile conquered the last Muslim stronghold in Christendom, the city of Granada. The Arabs were gone from the European continent.

In hindsight, this rejection can be seen as a lack of vision; the Europeans rejected a civilization that could have brought them much earlier the benefits of "trigonometry, astronomy, …, the corpus of Greek philosophy"[34]. More important, for centuries they had refused a society that could have helped them to link reason and religion, philosophy and theology, science and measured development.

The Europeans preferred to throw themselves in another adventure, the one we know very well. That same year in 1492,

Ferdinand and Isabella helped their Genovese protégé Christopher Columbus to set sail in search of a new route to the Indies... The Europeans may not have taken advantage of Muslim civilization while it was at their doorstep, but they still owe much of their Renaissance to Arab learning, even if the Western history books very rarely mention the role of the Islamic scholars in their culture.

Since the end of the fifteen century, five hundred years of discoveries and technical innovations have scientifically transformed the planet into an intricate ego-system. Through science, Man has developed a belief in himself. Science has come onto the scene with the force of a religion, but without any wisdom.

Today we know that at the beginning of the fifteenth century, the Chinese were already sailing around Asia and Africa in large ships; we also know that the Chinese, the Muslims and the Indians had established sufficiently coherent scientific foundations and economic systems to enable them to undertake significant technological developments. But their societies showed restraint and they did not throw themselves down the same path of technology that the Europeans took. Were they perhaps afraid of being unable to control their destiny? Their societies were ruled by order and harmony. The quest for a new way of life would certainly have brought material improvements, and other intellectual satisfactions too, but it might also have introduced changes jeopardizing a social order and philosophical balance that had taken centuries to develop. Because people felt secure in a stable society, there was no need to seek a more promising future through change – or Development as we are too inclined to call it.

The walls of Cluny whispered nothing about all of this.

In the years prior to my entering this monastery for educating engineers, I spent a lot of time studying philosophy. I naively thought that philosophical discussion was an integral part of any decision concerning the future of society. I was convinced that schools that prepared young people to lead and develop their country would include such discussion in the curriculum. At Cluny, there was rarely any mention of Plato, Hume, Kant, Auguste Comte or Bergson. The school was tasked with preparing us to enter industry and it delivered the necessary knowledge for us to do this. It was not responsible for helping us to define a way of life and still less a way of thought other than how to best exploit everything of value on earth. Values of existence had no place in an engineering school. Progress was our destiny. I had no qualms about taking this direction. It was only much later that I would come to realize that the industrial world would need to set limits on its Development.

When that happens – and it will happen in the very near future – the constraints that will be imposed on us will again seem unjustified to the sectarian followers of blind Development. In the twenty-first century, existential considerations will confront the pursuit of industrial development. The issues that Peter the Venerable and his friend Abelard debated, regarding the philosophy of existence and the role of science and its application, will arise again. Perhaps we will also try to find out why the 15th century Chinese, Indians and Muslims did not wish to pursue technological progress.

The years spent in that engineering school did not quench my thirst for scientific knowledge. In 1956, France discovered an important oil field in Hassi Messaoud, in the middle of the Sahara desert, and the idea of a career in the petroleum industry suddenly seemed attractive to me. The French Institute of Petroleum was the best French school for embarking on such a career and it would certainly propel me towards one of the coaches on the Train. By the time my class graduated we were impatient to start cracking the most compact molecules of petroleum to render them suitable for the dazzling feats that modern society might require of them. In short, we were ready to build sophisticated petrochemical plants and we were just waiting for an invitation from a company in order to do so.

At this Institute, just as at Cluny, the question of the harmful effects that industrial developments might have on the equilibrium of the environment was never raised; just as today's society does not dare to concern itself about the repercussions that our space developments might have on the equilibrium of the solar system. For me, as for my colleagues at the time, the size of the earth was simply not an issue, and so there was no reason to be concerned about the equilibrium of life on land and in the sea. The only elements that might alter the physiology of the earth would come from the earth itself or from large meteorites; but certainly not from human activity. Nor was it never envisaged that the earth's resources, be they petroleum, iron, copper, cobalt, manganese, or even less, fresh water, could become a moral issue. The ephemeral nature of the exploitation of the earth's resources was totally obscured. The faith in science and technological development that drove the profession was supreme. For us young engineers, the Train was moving forwards on the basis of a belief that we never questioned.

Before we put ourselves at your service, refiners, we were already devoutly yours!

CHAPTER 13

The Clergy of Science

S ociety certainly incited me to take the Train of Progress but now I feel the need to clarify how I personally was able to turn the theories that I learned at school into industrial realities without ever questioning the appropriateness of my commitment.

In the petroleum engineering field, it is customary to ask young engineers to participate in the development of new processes. This kind of applied research constitutes good professional training in itself. This is why, a few weeks into my first job, I was invited to join a small team tasked with testing an experimental pilot unit in order to make the final adjustments on a new hydrocarbon desulphurization process. In this model installation, petroleum and hydrogen were heated to a high temperature and forced through several layers of a catalyst in a reactor. This process was supposed to extract the sulfur from the petroleum in the form of hydrogen sulfide (H_2S). Our task was to determine the optimum operating conditions for an industrial-sized plant using this new chemical technology.

Since this pilot unit had been built to test a new process we knew there would be some hitches, and indeed, problems were not long in arising. At the first experimental operation, we learned that the catalyst crumbled, blocking the smooth flow of the petroleum. This caused the pressure in the reactor to rise abnormally. Consequently, we had to stop the experiment frequently to clean the unit. We ended up by breaking up each experiment into several sets of tests, each lasting only a few hours. One of the operators, who was always the same, had to check the pressure variations during the test from a platform at the top of the reactor, about fifty feet tall. We did the same at ground level. If the pressure reached a critical level, the control system automatically stopped the whole unit. The operator on the platform could also stop it for any reason he judged necessary. The safety rules of the refinery stated that in the event of risk he was to jump immediately from his observation point instead of taking the ladder. For that reason he always attached himself to a fall arrester that was supposed to limit the speed of his fall to that of a parachutist. Every evening after work he laughingly admitted to me that he could not wait to get back to his laboratory in Paris. I knew, however, that in reality, just like everyone involved in the project, he wanted to stay until the results of our tests were conclusive.

Our little team could not have been more active and enthusiastic during the four months of tests. We bustled about so determinedly that, if anyone had spied on us, he would have thought that the lives of a whole people depended on our work. The countless modifications to equipment, the cleanings, the laborious repeated start-ups and the tests of the installation were all part of our daily schedule. Nothing was too tedious for us.

The desulphurization technology that we tested proved to be excellent and in the years that followed it was adopted by refiners from all over the world. But we did not know this at the time and, if our main purpose had been to obtain valid results, it was not our only motive. For me personally, the technical functioning of each of the pieces of equipment was just as exciting as the chemical results that we were obtaining. There was no doubt that I was already hooked on Development. On my very first assignment, I boarded the Train of Progress. As for the oil that we were purifying, even if I knew its physical properties, I did not really identify it as fluid-bearing energy. For me, it was just a viscous black liquid whose qualities we were trying to improve. The ultimate beneficiaries of this new technology, the automobile owners and all the other consumers of oil products, never figured on my horizon, not even as the faintest speck.

A short time after this experience, I took part in the studies for and the construction of another experimental unit. This one was to develop an industrial process for producing synthetic isoprene. Its purpose was to replace the natural isoprene ($H_2C=C$ (CH_3)-$CH=CH_2$) found in the sap of the hevea tree, which was used to make rubber. Hevea forests could no longer satisfy demand and natural rubber was becoming rare and expensive. The trials for this pilot unit proved to be positive enough for a large oil company to invite us to study the technological and economic feasibility of an industrial-sized factory. Accordingly, for almost a year, we drew up detailed documents that would enable the refiner client to make his final decision concerning the development of the plant.

At the time that we presented our feasibility study to him, I was convinced that he would be in favor of building the big plant. I could not imagine how the world could do without such a promising tool as the one that we had just studied. In my mind, I could already see the new industrial facilities standing up on the site that had already been selected, near the Rhone River. There, where the river still has a blue-green hue from the Alpine rocks, I saw the huge reactors imposing themselves on the countryside and the chemical units gleaming against the sky.

When the client finally decided against building this plant, I felt overwhelming disappointment, almost incomprehension. It seemed to me that our client was clearly unable to fully appreciate the qualities of this new chemical process. It would have worked so well and would have given such excellent results! All of us who had taken part in the study would have loved to have built that factory. It was already in some way ours.

This disappointment, which might seem strange, proves to me that engineers cannot do without industrial developments. It is as if they are programmed to develop, whatever the consequences.

During the ensuing years, I often met researchers and engineers responsible for technological developments. Many had the good fortune to realize significant industrial applications such as high speed trains, satellite launchers or a new generation of submarines. I could see that they were all working with the same enthusiasm as I had. When their projects succeeded, they were delighted. When they failed, they were as disappointed as we were with our isoprene project. In Western society the paths of science and technology are noble paths. The individuals who follow them are convinced that they are working for the future, without ever really seeking to know what the ultimate consequences might be, without ever fearing that they might damage the future in some way. I am convinced that the people who developed the thermonuclear bomb felt deeply moved when it revealed its awesome power in the first test in the desert.

The scientists involved in technological developments place great hope in science. This hope goes well beyond reason. Their conviction is unaffected by any skepticism. They believe in what they are doing. They have a kind of faith in science; a faith that they never question; a faith that is all the greater for being shared by their whole working community. Scholars, scientists and engineers have become the clergy of the consumer society.

CHAPTER 14

The Camel-Drivers of Hassi R'Mel

The businessman: When you find a diamond that belongs to nobody in particular, then it's yours. When you find an island that belongs to nobody in particular, it's yours. When you're the first person to have an idea, you patent it and it's yours. Now I own the stars, since no one before me ever thought of owning them ...

The Little Prince: I own a flower myself which I water every day. I own three volcanoes, which I rake out every week .... So it's of some use to my volcanoes, and it's useful to my flower, that I own them. But you're not useful to the stars ...

Antoine de Saint-Exupéry [35]

After World War II, US corporations contributed to the rebuilding of Western Europe. In particular, they built refineries and chemical plants that were purposely sited to serve the main industrial centers. The companies that engineered them were also American. Even their equipment came from the United States. All of this was done within the framework of the Marshall Plan, which had been very favorably received on the Old Continent. The Plan helped the European countries to recover from the destruction that they had suffered and, at the same time, it gave them confidence in the future. But it also allowed American corporations to keep feeding work to their own factories in the United States. In the end, almost all the money put into the Marshall Plan by the Washington administration returned to the USA in one way or another. The main American oil companies, Aramco and the other "majors," who were aggressively exploiting the vast oil-fields recently discovered outside the United States, encouraged Europe to burn as many barrels of crude oil as possible. Their installations on European soil were excellent sources of profits for them. With crude oil valued at less than a dollar a barrel on the international market, it was easy to compete with coal and to persuade many consumers to use it instead. Their ego-systems were spreading their tentacles well beyond the North American continent.

By the late 1950s, some senior members of the French government felt that the US hegemony over oil on French soil had gone on long enough. They decided to set up a French engineering company that would build France's refineries and compete with the US companies. I was part of the group of young engineers who were to board that "coach" of the Train of Progress. It was not going to be easy. The entire oil industry viewed us at best as a premature baby – which was the opinion expressed by the French refining industry – or, worse, as an unwanted child – which was the view of the American engi-neering companies. To tell the truth, we may have had the pedigree of the French Institute of Petroleum but we had almost no industrial experience. In a world in which Rockefel-ler's Standard Oil Company had set down very professional engineering methods for decades we were just novices.

A short time after boarding this "coach" I was lucky enough to be placed on a team for my first real industrial project. A deposit of natural gas had recently been discovered at Hassi R'Mel in the Sahara, in the M'Zab region, and the exploration wells had indicated that it contained a substantial volume of gas. To date, it is still the largest deposit of natural gas to be exploited on the African continent. Our company was responsible for building the treatment plant that was to separate the natural gas – essentially methane (CH_4) – from the liquids associated with it. These included water, but also a large quantity of light liquid hydrocarbons that was close in composition to gasoline. The liquid hydrocarbons were to be sent two hundred miles south-east by pipeline to join the flow of petroleum coming from the Saharan oilfield of Hassi Messaoud. The natural gas, the primary product of the hydrocarbon field, was to be sent north in an enormous pipeline where it was to supply Algiers and the other major Algerian cities on the Mediterranean coast and also to feed into the gas exportation industrial complexes that were being set up near the ports.

When the time came to build the plant, I was sent to Hassi R'Mel to organize the start of the construction. It was August 1960, two years before Algeria became independent. Our Scrooge of a financial director had ordered a Citroen Deux-Chevaux to serve as the only vehicle for our whole site team – there would be nine of us at the peak. Because he placed the order too late for it to be shipped before the work began, it was decided that I would rent an automobile in Algiers and drive it to the site in the desert. Until the Deux-Chevaux arrived, my rental car would also be used as on-site transport for the other employees from our company.

I left Algiers in the middle of the night in a small white Renault Dauphine, which was quite classy but not at all equipped for the desert, which was scorching hot at that time of year and arrived at Hassi R'Mel at about three in the afternoon. For the last hours of the journey, I had been obliged to shut the windows of the car to keep the hot air from burning my face. I do not know what the temperature was inside the car but I felt as if I had been trapped in a sauna for many hours. When I finally arrived at the site, I discovered that the maximum official temperature that day had been 124°F. In addition to the unaccustomed heat, the road I was following was nothing more than barely discernible tracks in the sand. I was very pleased to have succeeded in reaching my destination without getting lost.

The base for my client's employees who were responsible for drilling for the gas was set on a huge barren plateau that was nothing but sand and rocks and it seemed to blend into the dunes. To escape the torrid heat everyone retired to his living quarters between noon and three. It was just as the camp was returning to work that I introduced myself to the operation manager. Before I had time to catch my breath he drove me round the wells that had already been drilled. They were scattered in a circle about sixteen miles in diameter around the point where our plant was to be erected. I wondered how he was able to find his way across the desert because a very strong wind had begun to blow, lifting the sand into the air. It obscured the ground and I had the impression that we were floating.

The exploration geologists had set up a concrete marker that showed, to the nearest millimeter, the geographical coordinates in latitude, longitude and altitude. Lost in the middle of a vast expanse of sand and stones stretching as far as the eye could see, this little dove-white post was to be our mark, as predators, on the desert. Using that almost sacred reference point, we were to build an industrial plant with equal precision. In the trackless immensity of the Sahara desert, this precision in itself bore all the arrogance of Northern industrialists.

The surrounding terrain was sandy and almost level, except for a few ravines, vestiges of the very rare rains. It was also extremely poor in plant life. You needed to lie flat on the ground to spot the faintest tinge of green. However, this meager vegetation, just a few tufts of very hardy grasses here and there, was enough to sustain a fauna barely detectable to the unsuspecting visitor. With a little attention, however, you could find a whole living world of animals there. Herds of gazelles with long slender legs moved across the horizon at the speed of desert winds. Desert foxes, with ears large enough to capture the sounds of the cosmos, hunted jerboas, little squirrel-like animals the color of the sun. Prehistory had also left a few iguanas there to start a new generation of dinosaurs when man's time has finally passed. Pending the arrival of this hypothetical but promising time, the stuffed skins of iguanas were displayed in the *souks* awaiting the few tourists who dared to travel to the distant oases and wanted a souvenir from the Sahara desert.

Eight months after my arrival, the plant was finished. The natural gas from the Hassi R'Mel field could now be treated so that the gas and liquid hydrocarbons could be sent out of the region through their designated pipelines. Throughout the construction there had been an excellent atmosphere on site. We had all experienced moments of intense activity as we adapted ourselves to the demands of the desert. We had shared good times and not so good times. We spent many moments in perfect communion, in particular during the sand storms. In severe storms, a very fine brick-red sand powder mixed with the air making it difficult to breathe. We had to lie down in the slightest depression that we could find and cover our faces with any clothing within reach. The habitués of the desert would share their fine cotton scarves with those who did not have one.

In the seemingly infinite desert I often felt like a being from nowhere. I was certainly not from the Sahara, but after several months in the desert I was no longer the out-and-out town-dweller who had arrived there the summer before. With no means of direct communication with the external world, we lived in a world apart. The workers on the site had all come from villages in the far north of the country and we did not have any contact with the Tuaregs who, with their camels, were the real people of the desert. No one of them ever participated in our great enterprise and not a single camel-driver ever came to visit us. Yet only one hour on foot from the site there was a well where the Tuaregs would water their mounts on their route across the sands. It was in fact the name of the well, Hassi R'Mel – "*hassi*" means "well" in the M'Zab language – that had been chosen as the name for the natural gas field. The Tuaregs took a track relatively close to our site but it was so little marked on the ground that personally I could never make it out. Their caravans rarely included more than five or six camels. I would sometimes watch their convoys through my binoculars. The slow, steady pace of the camels gave these travelers a stately appearance. I noticed that the camel-drivers did not deign to look at us. When we went to visit them at the well, we could not really converse with them for reasons of language but also because we were obviously of no interest to them. For the Tuaregs, we were part of an incomprehensible world, a world in which people had a different approach to existence. They knew that they would never be able to understand our thoughts, and still less our ideals, any more than we would be able to grasp theirs. They were equally indifferent to the installations that we were building, with their aluminum-colored parts glinting in the sun for miles around. They probably knew that we were in their desert to draw gas from its depths. They also probably knew that they could not prevent us from continuing our indelicate work. As for the gas itself, they attached no more significance to it than we do to the gas that makes up the atmosphere of the planet Jupiter.

The Tuaregs cut a noble figure on their camels. Their stylish wool and leather clothing probably changed little over time. Their attitude to their environment was completely different from ours. They lived in the desert in a natural way, they were a part of it; we considered it as something to be overcome. They loved it as a newborn babe loves its mother's breast; we exploited it, methodically. They lived in the present as a moment of eternity; we did not know how to live in the present but were hurtling towards a future that we wanted to change. Simply with their camels, traveling between the sand and stars, they were content. We, on the other hand, surrounded by a panoply of sophisticated equipment, were constantly seeking a contentment that is elsewhere, always further, always bigger.

Remembering the desert-dwellers today, I am convinced that they saw us as incapable of understanding their desert. It must have been difficult for them to imagine why we did not feel the need to live within our environment as it was. In this we must have seemed imbalanced in their eyes. And we were!

Today, I too ask myself fundamental questions about why we were there. The perception that I have now of the construction of the plant in Hassi R'Mel is not at all what it was when I was in this desert. I even go so far as to ask myself if we had the right to exploit the natural gas. Why did we do it? To deplete an organic product that had been there for millions of years with the sole objective of extracting as much of it as we could as quickly as possible? To give the populations of the North the temporary benefit of a gas whose magic powers would enable them to produce more equipment and set up increasingly sophisticated and powerful ego-systems? This, in turn would enable them to increase production and develop other ego-systems even better at damaging the habitat of us all, including those people who have not taken part in the kill?

During my eight months at Hassi R'Mel, it never occurred to me to ask myself these questions. Besides, strangely and even rather disturbingly for me today, I never imagined then that the gas flowing through our installations was in fact a source of energy responsible for maintaining our way of life. It was simply a substance like water, steel, aluminum or wood that Algeria and France needed.

I never knew where the camel-drivers passing through Hassi R'Mel really came from, nor where they were going. I never even tried to find out. This question is rather an absurd intellectual exercise anyway because even had I known the answer it would have meant nothing to me.

During my stay at Hassi R'Mel I had the opportunity to go a little further south, to Hassi Messaoud, where in 1956 the only significant oilfield ever exploited on "French" soil had been discovered. The field personnel lived in prefabricated metal housing that did not look like much from the outside but was extremely refined and comfortable within. It was set in a botanical park that had been created from scratch and was already quite dense in vegetation. It was in fact an artificial oasis! Its crystalline waters came from a deep aquifer that had been discovered by geologists while boring for oil. For these masters of the deep, the water was to be exploited in the same way as the hydrocarbons. Both had been specially stocked by the earth for those intelligent enough to find them. That was all there was to it.

Thinking now of the camel-drivers that I visited near the wells of Hassi R'Mel, I wonder if other camel-drivers will not, one day soon, have to take their mounts beyond the desert to find water.

CHAPTER 15

Trekking in Chad

In 1964 my company was chosen to develop an oil refinery in Abidjan, in the Ivory Coast, and I was to take part in its construction. The drawings, specifications and purchasing of equipment were all carried out by our Paris office. Meanwhile, locally, the future owner of the facilities had the tiny village nearby clear the site of the dense vegetation covering it. It was thus on a beautiful expanse of white sand between a lagoon and the sea that we were to start construction of the first oil refinery in the Ivory Coast.

Less than a year later, the project was completed and the refinery was ready to operate. During a brief opening ceremony we handed a symbolic key to the brand new director of the Société Ivoirienne de Raffinage. It was the first time in the world that an engineering company – ours – had taken complete financial responsibility for the entire construction of a refinery from start to finish. We could be quite satisfied with our achievement. And we were.

In that place, where previously monkeys had defied gravity jumping between the coconut palms, and where young Ivorians had come to capture boas to sell at the market in Abidjan, there was now a shiny new refinery and the endless drone of petroleum running through its pipes. This plant looked unreal in the landscape. It clearly did not belong to traditional Africa. Stuck there by Northern industry, it was detached from the present.

On my return to Paris, I was made responsible for all of my company's construction projects. Most of them were in countries that were either little, or not at all industrialized. There were not enough days in the month to visit all the construction sites. I would go from Morocco to Madagascar and from there to the delta of the Karnaphuli River in East Pakistan, which would become Bangladesh. I was almost always traveling and my suitcase sometimes had great difficulty keeping up with me on my many ports of call.

Very quickly I had begun to live and breathe the oil industry, traveling from country to country organizing the construction of industrial complexes that often constituted the first link in a chain of a new oil ego-system. I believed that I was helping to transfer technology to other countries and that seemed rather noble to me.

After two years of intense industrial activity, the first spent near Abidjan and the second making the rounds of construction sites of oil refineries in the most varied countries on the planet, I had the good luck to experience something completely different. A friend from the Ivory Coast invited me to accompany him on a five-week vacation to southern Chad to visit that country's most precious possession: nature in its pure state. My experience in the African bush would change drastically my way of looking at humanity. And the Earth itself.

Our guide who knew southern Chad well chose a place in the savanna that he had never explored and that was far from any material development. He was to be assisted by two trackers and an "aide-de-camp" whom he would hire from the village closest to our destination. Every day for five weeks we would follow only tracks that had been made by the animals themselves; there were no other tracks. We chose a campsite near a *bahr* – the name given to the rivers of the region – that only flowed during the wet season. As it was now the dry season of the year, the *bahr* had turned into a series of lakes of very different sizes and shapes. The largest could be quite long and often had hippopotami roaming submerged on the bottom. The smallest were no more than ponds and as the water disappeared the fish buried themselves in the mud to survive until the next rainy season. In some of the tiny pools the fish were so crowded together that the water would churn when we approached them.

The savanna, vast and untouched beyond the *bahr*, extended from clearing to clearing. The trees, shaped like giant parasols, were majestic. Still and silent, they seemed to be meditating. But it was the fauna that was the most striking. I had not thought that animals could be so numerous. I soon felt that I had been transported to a place that I had never even imagined. There, the world belonged to animals and to nature. Man was just one more inhabitant amongst many others. As a species, he was perhaps the least represented in terms of numbers and was not necessarily the best adapted. The true masters of the savanna were the big carnivores. They created a permanent state of fear that hung over all the animals and over the villagers too. The deer moved about in very large herds. It was their way of protecting themselves from their predators. The buffalo and wildebeest also stayed in herds. Animals with more solitary habits, such as the warthog, had no other means of discouraging their predators than to remain on the move or hide. Even the elephants watched attentively over their young until they were fully grown.

As for the representatives of *Homo sapiens*, they shut themselves away in their little villages consisting of a few straw huts surrounded by solid hedges. These hamlets were few in number and spaced at least twenty miles apart. The men only left them to go hunting armed with spears. The women did not dare venture outside except to fill their gourds at the nearest watering place.

The lakes and their banks were often covered with ducks, waders, cranes and many other birds. The spectacle of thousands of birds in flight was enthralling. It was impossible to take in anything other than their cries and the flapping of their wings as huge colonies of cranes and black storks took to the sky in the course of just a few minutes. We observed them without talking. We could not have heard each other over the noise anyway.

There was no doubt about it: we were not on an earth of men alone. The omnipresence of animals made me think of how most of the continents must have been just a few thousand years ago.

Once the rain returned and the river started flowing again and the natural grasslands were again covered with tall grasses, the region would be inaccessible to humans. At that time of year, travel was so difficult that the villagers very rarely left their huts, so great was the chance of being ambushed by some wild beast hiding in the vegetation. These villagers totally fascinated me. Because they had not been influenced by modern life they seemed to be true representatives of the human race, while we were just some rather disturbing element artificially added to the landscape. In the presence of this nature, at once so rich and so cruel, we did not seem natural. Nowhere else have I ever had such a strong feeling of being an outsider. The environment, with all it comprised, seemed as pure to me as a starlit sky. Yet this was no haven of peace. Quite the contrary. Before this trip, I could never have imagined that there existed on earth a place where direct predation was the only way of existing and also the primary activity of every species, including our own. The natives there lived isolated from the rest of the world. Each village had its own language and its people were not aware of belonging to a nation. It is unlikely that they had ever even heard the name of the one in which they lived. For them, boundaries were made by vegetation, rivers and animals. They knew no others.

There are very few places still existing on earth as untouched as the savanna that I had had the chance to know in Chad. Every country seemed to make it a point of honor to make such places disappear, and this is due more to the rush to exploit the existing resources than to help the inhabitants. This part of Chad had been fortunate enough to remain natural. The industrialized countries had not yet found natural resources to exploit and its inhabitants still faced their own destiny.

Our visit passed without major incident although on certain outings, in particular when overly energetic animals came too close for my liking, I was not altogether at ease. For safety, the guide carried a gun but frankly, against some of the elephants, this would have been about as much use as a sling-shot. We trekked single file through the savanna during the day and at night we slept in camp beds set up under the stars with nothing but a mosquito net for protection. It would have been difficult to have had closer contact with nature, even if fear of the lions prevented me from sleeping for most of the first four nights there. Any meat that we caught during the day was cured over an open fire at night in the camp and the smell of it attracted lions and other big cats, which roared so loudly they might have been under my bed. To deter them, our helpers kept a few fires burning and throw glowing embers in their direction. Apparently this trick was enough to dissuade them from coming any closer but I was never really convinced of this.

I was sorry that the day to leave had come so soon. You cannot really know a region until you have been part of it for some time, which was clearly not yet the case for me in Chad. For the inhabitants of that place, we were probably never anything more than imposters traipsing clumsily across their beautiful savanna. For my part, I only understood what my limited means of perception as a "developed" European had allowed me take in. It was certainly far from reality. There was a whole world between the authentic inhabitants of that savanna and us visitors: that of nature.

After we left the savanna I wondered if we had been right to go there. I feared that just the presence of our little group in that place, even if we always stayed prudently quite far away from the villages, might have engendered a feeling of covetousness in its inhabitants. Had we not borrowed our trackers from them, the village would not have had any contact with outsiders and the very character of the natural life of the place would not have been violated. The harmony that reigned between the savanna, its animals and the natives showed that nature was respected; that each species had a chance to live its own life and play its role in the equilibrium of the place. The villagers lived off fishing, hunting and gathering and, even if they grew a few cassavas in their village, they never felt the need to hoard everything around them, and still less to change the nature of their environment. They were true inhabitants of the earth. In their world, from photosynthesis to the lion's roar, everything was preserved. It was certainly what made me instinctively respect that place.

I also wondered how that little part of Chad would end up. It seemed unthinkable to me that the West would not get round to it one day. I could also easily imagine that when this time came, the Development would not be carried out with much tact and that not much time would be given to these populations to adjust to what would seem to them to be the end of the world. Indeed this Development would in fact be the end of the world that they knew, the world that, for them, made sense. I was convinced that the developers who approached them would move too fast for their preservation. Even impersonal technological methods might be used to take care of them like those gigantic machines whose arms rip out the Amazonian rainforest and blindly destroy nature without giving their inhabitants anything of value in exchange. When this happens, some of the last *Homo sapiens* living in balance with nature will be gone forever.

It did not in fact take long for the plunderers of natural resources to make their appearance. Towards the end of the 1990s several foreign oil operators obtained prospecting licenses for Chad and some of them did find deposits of black gold. Since 2003, a pipeline shared by ExxonMobil, Chevron-Texaco and Petronas, a Malaysian company, have been exporting oil from there to the "developed" nations. The people of Chad will not be able to count on this energy in the future. They cannot even really benefit from it today. The meager royalties that the oil companies pay the Chad government do not represent the real value of the product that they are rapaciously seizing, almost like thieves.

The pipeline starts two hundred miles from the place where I trekked in 1964. It is possible that the little bit of nature that I explored then will be preserved for a short while longer, but the tentacles of ego-systems greedy for natural resources will have no scruples in wiping it out – for good – should they discover any trace of some new resource to exploit to exhaustion.

CHAPTER 16

Why so Fast?

Though I don't know where we are going,
I am sure we are going faster

Chris Newbery[36]

When I returned to Paris from Chad, my mind was full of conflicting images of two completely opposite worlds. Visions of the mysterious, beautiful and natural savanna jostled with those of the most presumptuous technological developments of industry. I could not understand how, in some parts of the world, human beings could still live free from all material trappings. I also could not understand how we in the West had come to live in concrete jungles removed from any natural context. These images provoked existential questions in me that I found hard to convey to other people and I think this was why I kept the essence of my experience in Chad to myself. I was sure of one thing, however, and that was that for each of the two worlds, the other remained esoteric. Neither had any chance of understanding the motivations or aspirations of the other.

While I was trekking through the savanna, every moment of the day took on natural meaning. Logically this experience ought to have slowed down my race for Progress. But this was not at all what happened. Almost straight away, I was caught up again in the Development game. Worse still, I learned to use my memories of Chad which I could call on at any time to reassure me. They reminded me that, in some remote part of the world, human beings still lived a basic life. Subconsciously, they gave me faith in mankind and helped me to tolerate the most questionable aspects of my job.

Paradoxically, they helped me to persevere with my work as a "developing" engineer. Once again, I began to live and breathe industry. In the following years, I took part in technical projects in France, Africa and Asia that were even more convoluted than refineries. These included offshore oil platforms and chemical factories. Our accomplishments seemed positive to me, so I felt no need to open myself up to some deeper contemplation.

Looking back on that period now I can perceive that, intellectually, I craved technological developments like a drug. Of course, I did not see it like that at the time. I did not ask myself if the projects were taking society in the right direction. I freely abandoned myself to that "drug." Without knowing it, I fundamentally belonged to a powerful ego-system.

There were those, however, even some very close to us, who were upset to see us acting so obstinately. A memorable example of this occurred during a trip in Iran with the manager of my company and our wives. We had just left Persepolis where we had spent part of the day admiring the ruins of the ancient Persian capital, and were heading towards Shiraz, the city that inspired the great Persian poets Saadi, Firdusi and Omár Kháyyám. The arid landscape was stunningly beautiful. The pastel colors of the mountains at sunset seemed to have been painted by a ray of magical light. We could not stop extolling the beauty of it all when suddenly a gleaming chemical factory appeared on the horizon. The contrast between the natural beauty of the place and this massive metal structure could not have been more shocking. Immediately a silence fell on us, only to be broken by the wife of my senior manager, who completely taken aback by what she had just seen, suddenly blurted out the word, "Bastards!" From her expression I could tell that she was referring to both of us engineers, even if we had not personally been responsible for that industrial fertilizer-producing "heap" that had been built by a competitor of our company. A single word uttered by that lady of impeccable manners had "written off" the work that others had carried out with much dedication. Our long silence indicated that we agreed with her, but she remained no less upset for the remainder of the evening. She had suddenly seen the reality of the type of work in which her husband and I were involved, in Iran and elsewhere; and the types of installations that "developed" countries were building to procure a life of luxury for their populations. Maybe she even felt betrayed by the society in which she lived.

Today, I can still hear her exclamation of distress. The landscape that triggered it is engraved in my memory, as are the images of the virgin savanna in Chad. These memories do not only evoke the past; they question and challenge me. They demand that I justify my conduct over so many years as an indefatigable industrial engineer. When I look back at my professional career, I feel uncomfortable. Sometimes I even feel appalled that I was able to rush through project after project without any qualms. Knowing how my grandparents had always lived so simply and traditionally, I wonder how, in just two generations, I had come to crave complexity to such an extent that I would derive pleasure from building large industrial plants using ultra-sophisticated technology. How could I have made such a leap towards the material, sometimes even virtual, world? Why had I so willingly dismissed the wisdom of those who lived peacefully on their little mountain in Auvergne?

Obviously I am not alone in this technological adventure. There are millions of us. Countless Americans, the grandchildren of those who were forced to take on the most unpleasant jobs simply to survive in the Great Depression that followed the Crash of 1929, have in just two generations become the builders of some of the most sophisticated equipments and networks in the world. The question is a general one: how have we all, or almost all, in the West been able to go so fast, and without really thinking it through? How have we gone in the space of a few generations from a time when men were relatively calm and connected to nature, to a time when the most excessive developments, some even without a future, can be carried out? Why do we still race towards the future as if it were some sort of gold rush?

Nine thousand years separate the time that the inhabitants of the Fertile Crescent built their first cities, like Catal Huyuk and Jericho, from the West's Industrial Revolution. How can it be that we have managed to cover the earth in just a little more than a century with our extraordinary but unsustainable ego-systems? Why, after Descartes gave us so much confidence in our powers of reason, have we done this with so little forethought?

Given the speed with which we have made this journey, it would have been impossible for us not to have erred. In fact, we were bound to make plenty of mistakes. If nature requires thousands of years to carry out often minor evolutions, there is no way that in just a few generations we can carry out major developments without jeopardizing the equilibrium of our society and the equilibrium of life itself.

Unfortunately, it is no longer a question of probability. The damage is already done. I will take two examples, both related to the sea. The first one concerns oyster fishing:

> In the Chesapeake Bay ... agricultural development in the 18th and 19th centuries had very little impact on water quality, despite increased runoff into the Bay from cleared land. The active filtering of vast numbers of oysters was said to have cleaned the entire water column of the Bay every three to six days. But with the advent of mechanical oyster dredges in the 1870s and the decimation of the oyster population through overfishing, Bay water quality began to decline rapidly, and to lose the dissolved oxygen that is critical to all marine life. Today, at only two per cent of their historic numbers, oysters in the Bay take more than a year to filter the same amount of water.[37]

The second one takes place in the northern Pacific Ocean. Because we are not careful enough about their ultimate destination, many of the plastic objects that we throw away end up in the rivers and finally in the sea. Plastic debris reaching the Pacific Ocean is carried hundreds of miles by ocean current to an immense whirlpool – the North Pacific Gyre – spinning clockwise in about half way between San Francisco and the Hawaiian Islands. This phenomenon has created a body of plastic trash that is probably bigger than Texas, Germany or France, is 300 feet deep at its center and is estimated to weigh tree million tons. Although this soupy mass is made up mostly of fine plastic chips that come from all types of equipment and packaging, it also contains larger objects, from plastic bottles, diapers, toys, disposable cigarette lighters to fishing nets and even parts of automobiles. It is so big that it is unimaginable that it could be cleaned up by Man in the future. Meanwhile world production of plastics continues to grow. Growth is part of Progress.

This monstrous "garbage sea-dump" is killing the pelagic birds that fish there. Jean-Michel Cousteau, President of the Ocean Futures Society, during a reconnaissance mission to the Pacific in 2004, found that the beaches in the North Western Hawaiian Islands were covered with the corpses of albatrosses. They had starved to death, their stomachs stuffed with plastic garbage.

There are thousands of other equally alarming cases. In every sector that our ego-systems have exploited, the future of the living world has become a concern. In the face of these "disasters" – the word is certainly a euphemism – we must try to find some explanation. We must try to understand why industry promotes crazy methods to achieve its ends; why the economy builds ephemeral ego-systems that destroy the earth's equilibrium; why, we risk sacrificing life just to satisfy our immediate whims.

Why are we going so fast?

CHAPTER 17

Counter to Culture

The invasion of southern Chad by the oil companies that I have described earlier illustrates the extent of the arrogance of our "developed" world and its blindness to the beauty of existence. The natural unspoiled villages there had their future stolen from them, almost for fun. Just to enable a few groups of privileged people, living on the other side of the world, to wallow in a little more excess. Just to allow factories to produce still more. Just to keep gardeners with their leaf-blowers busy on the lawns of California.

I imagine that when the petroleum engineers, with all their mechanical paraphernalia, first burst into the villages of Chad the villagers had no words to describe what was happening. They were certainly "crushed" by the intrusion.

When I think of the grief caused to these people I cannot help but recall the anxiety expressed by the inhabitants of places where I myself, with my colleagues, had come to build industrial complexes that the locals did not necessarily want.

After Algeria obtained its independence from France in 1962, the government in Algiers, determined to push the country into industrial development, set up long-term plans for the country. In 1967, I was sent to Algeria to manage the construction of two industrial plants that were supposed to generate the country's Development: an ammonia (NH_3)

fertilizer plant in the west of the country and a plant for the liquefaction of natural gas (methane CH_4) in Kabylie, in the east. The raw material needed to supply the two petrochemical plants was the natural gas that originated in the Sahara desert at Hassi R'Mel, a place I knew particularly well.

Both projects were huge and technically difficult. In the first, some equipment operated at temperatures higher than 2000°F (1100°C) while other equipment worked under very high pressure. In the second, the natural gas had to be cooled at the cryogenic temperature of -260°F (-162°C) to be liquefied. My company had agreed to take on great financial risk in a politically unstable country. The construction of these two projects would thus require my close attention, which was not a bad thing as far as I was concerned.

A few months after my arrival, I was surprised to hear the charismatic Minister of Work and Industry Abdelaziz Bouteflika – future President of Algeria – proudly announce on television, "We will stick to this four-year plan, even if it takes ten years."

During the time that I spent there, I did everything in my power to ensure that the two projects were carried out in the best interests of the Algerians. Nevertheless, I often had the impression that these undertakings went against the wishes of the people. The national company in charge of the country's hydrocarbons only very rarely deigned to share its plans for Algeria's future with the local representatives affected by the developments. This is why, very reluctantly, I finally had to deal directly with the local administration on each site, that is, the Sub-Prefect, the Chief Prosecutor of the Algerian Republic, the Customs Director, the Mayor, the Chief of Police and the Port Director. It became my job to persuade them of the administrative, technical, and occasionally even political, appropriateness of our projects so that I could obtain their support as needed. I even had to deal with the Algerian army, which the government in Algiers had sent to grade the site for the liquefaction plant.

The local populations had great difficulty accepting the technical developments that the authorities in Algiers were imposing on them; in fact, they had barely been informed about these plants. Many of them did not see industrial development as a panacea. The government was asking them to adapt to high speed industrial development that could not be carried out with the same intensity across every sector of activity and every level of society, when most of the people did not have the bare minimum of comfort in their homes. Many did not even have running water or electricity. They sensed that the modernity being imposed on them was inextricably linked to the exploitation of their country and they were certain that the way of life, so beloved by the West, was not for them. It was beyond their intellectual understanding, against their culture, and at times, contrary to the very ideals that they had upheld in their fight for independence. They would have preferred a society that respected their past.

Now, years later, I have great difficulty explaining my enthusiasm for those projects. What I took to be important industrial projects for the future of Algeria were, in reality, just huge, metal, technological monsters from another world that had been dumped on the local citizens by foreign companies. Nothing they had ever known was as technically complicated as the industrial plants that we had just built on their land. Without realizing it – and this is certainly no excuse – we were imposing our type of Development on the Algerian people for our own purposes. We acted with a self-assurance that was only equaled by our ignorance of the real aspirations of the Algerian people. When "developed" countries impose their industry on another country, they show their lack of respect for the culture of those people. This has become increasingly true. Globalization, promoted as bringing wealth to those who adopt its principles, is in fact organized primarily in favor of the businesses of the rich nations.

Average Europeans and Americans know little about the cultures of Third World countries. They think that Muslims, in particular, maintain a way of life closed to scientific and real

Progress. Western societies want to believe that the Muslim world is backward because it does not embrace the industrial path. But it is possible that the Muslims want to know where our path is leading before taking it. Perhaps they do not want to venture into the unknown. Or perhaps they already know that it would be wiser not to follow us. We ourselves still do not know where this path is taking us. As Karen Armstrong says in *The Battle of God*, "there was no real incompatibility between Islam and the West. ... It was only when Western modernity replaced the backward-looking mythical way of life with a future-oriented rationalism that some Muslims would begin to find Europe alien."[38] For Muslims, "Education ... consisted largely of rote learning and did not encourage originality. Students were not taught to conceive radically new ideas, because the society could generally not accommodate them; such notions could, therefore, be socially disruptive and endanger a community. In a conservative society, social stability and order were considered more important than freedom of expression."[39]

In the West, we uphold the opposite principle. We believe that stability and harmony are irrelevant and outdated values. We have opted for change through research and technology. We have dogmatically boarded the Train of Progress.

Throughout my stay in Algeria, I was convinced that I was working for the good of the country and I never appreciated the extent to which the Algerian people resented our way of organizing their future. I was just serving the ego-systems of Progress of the North. An engineer's faith in what he is doing, however real, is not necessarily honest. Immersed in industrial society, he does not have the latitude to reflect on the deeper significance of his work. He is not encouraged to assess the need for any particular project. His approach is certainly not philosophical; it is above all ego-systematic.

Part III

The Fate of the Industrial Wave

CHAPTER 18

All Things Wear Away

I want none of a world where nothing can stay
Where all things, even memory, wear out and wear away

Lamartine [40]

I ndustry has taken on an amazing role. It has – peremptorily – seized the right to lead the world. The pioneers of industry, confident as they were at the outset, could probably not have imagined that nations would adopt technological development so rapidly and unreservedly. Today, the countries that dominate the world cannot function without industry as a partner. Industry is as fundamental to our type of western society as seal hunting is to the Inuit of Greenland. Our adherence to the industrial order is so profound that very few of us are ready to admit that material development might one day be suspended. We prefer to deny that the Train of Progress could ever slow down. It is unimaginable to us. Progress is synonymous with the future; and the future, like time, is something that never stops.

The advances made by the pioneers of industry were for a long time attributed just to their talents as inventors of new technologies and too rarely to the principle behind them, which was the mastery of energy in their engines. Without ergamines, society would not be where it is today. Without the ability to put them to work in engines and power plants, we would have stayed with our draught animals and our windmills and have been unable to set up the ego-systems that control the world. Thanks to a plethora of energy, countries acquire the industrial power that determines their place on the world scene. Depending on whether they turn the cogs of industry a lot, a little, or not at all, they are classed as "developed countries," "developing countries" or "undeveloped countries."

The quantity of energy used by humans has reached a phenomenal, even unimaginable, level. In the so-called "developed" countries, excessive use of ergamines has become the rule; it determines the standard of living.

Until now, it has been the custom to measure the use of energy in terms of consumption, but it would be more honest to measure it in terms of depletion. For, we are in fact very systematically exhausting the reserves. The day that Man began digging for coal or drilling for oil and natural gas, he should have loudly sounded the bugle that he was going in for the kill.

In many European countries the process of depleting these finite resources is admirably running its course. In France, the hunt is already over, the quarry is killed. With just a few exceptions, all of the fossil deposits have been exhausted throughout the territory. This achievement has taken place with the complete complicity of the engineers of France's main public services.

What is happening in Western Europe is also taking place all over the world. The day is coming when energy obtained from fossil deposits will no longer be enough to sustain industrial society. The production of fossil fuels worldwide is about to reach a historic peak after which it will no longer meet the demand. For the first time in history, nature will not be able to provide sufficient ergamines to satisfy the energy needs of nations on a global scale.

When fossil fuels start to run out, there will be no magic potion to substitute for them in sufficient quantities. Industrialized countries will be obliged to invest more in harnessing alternative sources of energy, in particular solar power, but all of the non-fossil sources combined will not provide enough additional fuel to prevent the world from suffering a major energy shortage. Industrialized nations will face a major restriction on their ego-systems and a lower standard of living. Their power is, after all, rooted in dependency on energy.

Designed to run mostly on non-renewable fuel, ego-systems are ephemeral. "Developed" countries can no longer hide from the truth: their society is ephemeral. Modern society will soon realize that it is heading inexorably towards a hellish decline.

The nations that chose the industrial path would have been wise to plan for the exhaustion of fossil resources over the long term, or even the very long term, several millennia. Instead they let the oil companies, and their related businesses, enter the relentless competitive game leading to the total depletion of these magic substances as quickly as possible. Crude oil well deserves its nickname, "black gold." It is sought with as much passion if not more as yellow gold.

Governments, rather than preparing their people for the coming energy crisis, are promoting "political" fuels instead to justify their own power. Hydrogen is one of them. Unfortunately, there are no reserves of free hydrogen on earth. It occurs mostly in combination with oxygen or carbon and must be extracted from water or from hydrocarbons. The process of producing hydrogen in significant quantities requires the consumption of two to three times more energy than can be obtained from hydrogen fuel itself. In addition, it is so volatile that it is very difficult to contain. Whenever it is in its free state, it leaves the earth and returns home to the universe. But these drawbacks do not seem to alter politicians' faith in hydrogen; celebrating the cult of the car is always appreciated by the electorate.

During the California gubernatorial campaign of 2003, Arnold Schwarzenegger promised that, if elected, he would build hydrogen fueling stations at 20-mile intervals along California's major highways. In April 2004, during a visit to the University of California at Davis, the new master alchemist reaffirmed his positive goal, "He said, 'I will sign an executive order creating a public-private partnership creating hydrogen highways all over the state of California by the year 2010. Hundreds of hydrogen fueling stations will be built. And these stations will be used by thousands of hydrogen-powered cars and trucks and buses. This starts a new era for clean California transportation.' "[41]

At the end of February 2006, during a visit to an experimental hydrogen project in Chico, California, President G.W. Bush himself prophesized, "Hydrogen fuel cells represent one of the most encouraging, innovative technologies of our era. ... if you are tired of the same old endless struggles that seem to produce nothing but noise and high bills, let us promote hydrogen fuel cells as a way to advance into the 21st century. If we develop hydrogen power to its full potential, we can reduce our demand for oil over 11 million barrels per day by the year 2040."[42] Such divination! If his prophecy were to come true the energy that would be produced by hydrogen fuel cells in the United States in 2040 would equal half of all the fossil fuel energy the country burned in 2007. The master magician from Washington was not to be outdone by the master alchemist from California.

The hydrogen prognostications made by American politicians are so preposterous that even the Pythia of Delphi, who willingly gave the most favorable prophecies on behalf of Apollo, would have been astonished to hear them.

A second substitute energy that is getting considerable political mileage in several countries at the moment is biofuels. In Paris, in May 2006, the French Finance Minister Thierry Breton urged automobile manufacturers to equip their vehicles with engines that can run on both biofuels and conventional gasoline or diesel. "It would be good if by 2010 each consumer had a real choice between biofuels and classic fuels," were his words.

The biofuels that many countries are already producing, in particular in France and the United States, are derived from plants rich in calories. They include oleaginous plants, sugar beets, corn and sugar cane.

Turning these crops into petrochemical fuels is not without severe consequences. Nearly any conversion of agricultural products to biofuels is made at the expense of the production of food for humans, or livestock which ultimately comes to the same thing. To promote biofuels is thus to prioritize the feeding of cars over the feeding of people. It is difficult to imagine a greater abuse against humanity. In October 2006, Jacques Diouf, Director-General of the FAO (Food and Agriculture Organization of the UN) said, "A decade after the 1996 World Food Summit in Rome, where nations promised to reduce the number of undernourished people by half by 2015, there are 20 million more – [increasing the total to] 820 million – than there were then." In late February 2008, the FAO announced that the price of wheat was more than 80 percent higher than a year before, and corn prices were up by 25 percent. In the United States alone, 14 percent of the corn crop was transformed in biofuel in 2006. It is expected to reach 30 percent in 2010. Cereals and corn have really become a source of fuel. Consequently their price is now directly linked to the price of crude oil. The FAO estimates that the cereal import bill of the neediest countries will increase substantially again in 2008. This will reduce considerably the number of people that can be fed through its World Food Program.

According to Lester R. Brown, "In agricultural terms, the world appetite for automotive fuel is insatiable. The grain required to fill a 25-gallon SUV gas tank with ethanol will feed one person for a year. The grain to fill the tank every two weeks over a year will feed 26 people. Investors are jumping on the highly profitable biofuel-bandwagon ..."[43] It should be added that the production of biofuels requires itself such large quantities of fuel that the net energy yield is very often less than one-fifth of the energy consumed to grow and process it. In other words, the amount of grain required to fill that SUV gas tank every two weeks over a year should be increased five fold. It would feed in reality more than one hundred people.

Neither can we ignore the effect that a substantial use of biofuels will have on the natural ecosystems. Fields of crops for biofuels are, in effect, man-made fields of hydrocarbons. Every time one of our agricultural fields becomes an "oil field," a new agricultural field has to be prepared and irrigated to replace the lost food production. Overall, the production of biofuels destroys the natural ecosystems that maintain the earth's equilibrium. And it increases the mass of CO_2 emitted into the atmosphere.

Modern society, like many individuals, has let itself be carried away by the quest for material progress concomitant by the drive for profit imposed by some, and almost always by the pursuit of corporate and national power.

The fateful energy drama is about to begin in a climate of general indifference.

But how has our society, which seems so sure of itself and so exceedingly competent, managed to be so unconcerned about its future? Why have the philosophers and scientists who, more than two centuries ago, led mankind out of the darkness and into the Enlightenment, led us indirectly to a dead-end? Has Western society gambled with Progress? Should we posthumously condemn Bacon, Galileo, Kepler, Hobbes, Descartes, Torricelli, Pascal, Huygens, Locke, Newton, and all the other great minds who placed us on this uncertain path? Or, did we misunderstand them? Did we allow ourselves to be convinced that science holds the answer to the future instead of verifying their assertions? After all, they were just men and, like us, liable to error. René Descartes came to champion the idea that animals cannot suffer because they have no mind, no soul, no language and no emotions.

By rushing too enthusiastically into the Enlightenment, Man believed that he had finally found his ultimate path, not to say "The Path" for some. The Renaissance had revealed him to be a Thinking Being. Now, science showed him that he had the appropriate Intelligence to discover the Universal Laws. He started to think that the Individual could exist independently of the constraints of established political order and religion. Through his Social Revolutions, he reached the level of personal Liberty. And he set off down the path of industrialization as naive and sure of himself as a fresh-faced boy soldier off to battle and eager for glory. In the end, he seems to have placed too much hope in himself and he fell into the trap of his inventions. He wanted the Industrial Revolution to shoot off like Halley's Comet and he strove hard to ensure that it did.

Soon, Western society could no longer do without drive belts, gear-wheels, hydraulic, combustion-driven pistons, accelerators, and electrical motors. The Industrial Revolution was hailed as the "Future." Diderot wrote, "Thanks to the works of these great men, the world is no longer a god; it is a machine which has its wheels, its cords, its pulleys, its springs and its weights."[44] Man wanted to dominate the World. He was even prepared to make it anew.

The Knights of Industry opened their doors to an ever increasing number of increasingly skilled workers. These workers were exploited in every way although over time, sometimes over a very long time, they did learn to forge tolerable working conditions for themselves. Nevertheless, whether employers or employees, they all believed in Industry. Industry became the universal means of Development, as much in the East under the communist regime as in the West under the democratic regimes that promote free enterprise.

Through Industry, we asserted ourselves over the planet. We managed to dominate nature. We acquired a new life-force and we became powerful. The whole of society became powerful. Ultra-powerful. Too powerful.

We believed that we were as free as the gods of Mount Olympus to do as we pleased with the world. But our freedom turned out to be a double-edged sword. We have certainly acquired massive power, but through our excessive ambitions, we have debased it.

Industrial society is surfing precariously on a dangerous Energy Wave. Despite warning signs, it continues to consume with an almost insane greed every profitable resource within its reach. If the inhabitants of the "developed" countries cared to look at the horizon, they could already glimpse the reefs on which their ego-systems will founder. But, engrossed by the race for luxuries available at the flip of a switch, their society is trapped and they fail to see the dangers ahead.

All things wear out and wear away, even power.

CHAPTER 19

The Energy Wave

We civilizations, we now know that we too are mortal

Paul Valéry [45]

The energy curve set out on the graph below combines the three main types of energy, fossil, nuclear and renewable, consumed worldwide and projects their use for the present century (See Appendix B for the details). The curve, which has the profile of a wave, is highly significant. This Energy Wave illustrates that our industrial society is heading towards the exhaustion of the fuels that sustain it.

The Energy Wave which is carrying the world is so gigantic that, compared to it, the power derived from human labor represents nearly nothing, less than 0.1% of the physical work that keeps the society running. If human labor was shown on this graph, its line would be thinner than that of the horizontal axis.

Like any wave, the Energy Wave will pass and go away. For two centuries, it has been steadily rising. It might crest in around the year 2020. After that fateful event, the availability of energy worldwide will begin its inexorable "descent." To deny this fact would be as unreasonable as refusing to believe that mountains have peaks.

The descent will cause immeasurable upheaval in the world and will result in profound changes to our society. If, as the Energy Wave was rising, the industrialized nations gained affluence and power – enormous power – it follows that as it falls, this affluence and power will decrease.

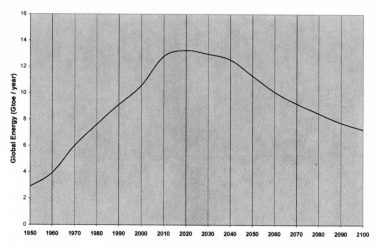

Global Energy Consumption Wave

Gtoe = gigatons of oil equivalent per year

The Energy Wave actually "supports" the industrial power of the "developed" countries. Indeed it "supports" the whole of industrial civilization. The global industrial power moves also up and down like a wave in parallel with the Energy Wave. The Global Industrial Wave will peak at the same time as the Energy Wave crests. Our "developed" world is almost on the brink of this decline, and yet, rather than face the imminence, it still prefers to believe that mountains have no peaks.

During the twenty-first century our ego-systems will be turned upside down. Many will not survive. We, the people, are just as much to blame as our politicians. We never want representatives to ask us to moderate our enthusiasm for our sacrosanct Development. We have the leaders that we deserve and cannot exonerate ourselves.

The Energy Wave set out here assumes that society will not panic and fight over ever decreasing resources. This will almost certainly not be the case in reality. If after 2010 the energy shortage leads to chaos in the industrialized world, the Wave may take on a very different shape. It may even break before cresting.

The effects of energy restriction will not be felt across the world in the same way and reactions will be varied and often conflicting. Countries that are dependent on other countries for fossil fuels are likely to be the first to suffer. Some will even use their armies to restrict access to their sources of hydrocarbons. Some industrialized nations may even collapse in the confusion.

Looking at American society today you might think that it was born as an "energivore" in the same way that elephants are born as herbivores. Its basic principle of linking time with money prevents it from realizing that the resources sustaining it – in particular hydrocarbons – are finite. Its housing, transport, and industry are organized on the never questioned postulate that the energy sources are inexhaustible.

We have already started to substitute coal, nuclear and solar energies for the diminishing hydrocarbons. These energies are suitable primarily for the production of electricity. American society, along with many others, will be forced to rely more heavily on Watts. Because electricity is difficult to store, it is less versatile in its use. As a result, a society that prioritizes the use of electricity requires more organization from the State, more leadership and less free enterprise, than a society that functions on hydrocarbons. The electric infrastructure in the United States is so outdated that it will be inadequate to ensure the necessary changeover to electricity.

For decades, American business has steered the country in the opposite direction. Many urban transport systems that ran on electricity have been dismantled. In San Francisco, only two of the city's 18 original cable car lines are still running, basically for tourists. The population of Los Angeles was even less fortunate; in the 1930s, General Motors purposely bought up the tramway companies and tore out the tracks to force the local population to acquire private vehicles. These are but two examples and the overall result is that most of the rail networks operating in the United States are mostly run on diesel and are antiquated. In Kazakhstan, many of them would probably be considered as relics of the past.

For countries that have chosen the industrial path, the fall of the Energy Wave will be painful and will affect almost every aspect of industrial production.

The various types of industrial production on which we depend: mining, manufacturing, agribusiness, fishing, transportation... will rise quickly, peak, and then decline in tandem with the Energy Wave. All are connected, directly or indirectly, to the Energy Wave. To make matters worse, many of them depend on raw materials that will become increasingly scarce due to the lack of energy. This will accelerate their decline.

The population will also decline. The increasing promotion of biofuels, which is already underway, is at the expense of food for humans. Every day, little by little, new developments reduce the amount of agricultural land available for growing food. Making humans compete with cars for food will go down in history as an indirect crime against humanity.

It is true that the Industrial Era has brought about an impressive series of improvements to human daily life, in particular in health and living standards, even if only a fifth of the world's population ever benefits from them. It has also increased our general knowledge. But, judged as the "civilization of excess" by posterity, our civilization will never be seen as brilliant. The generations who live after this time of plenty, which we enjoy so outrageously, will view the Industrial Revolution as an offence against life in general. We will leave permanent scars: the depletion of vital natural resources, mountains of waste (some of which will remain radioactive forever), layers of contaminated soil, seas polluted with chemicals and plastics, rings of debris orbiting the globe, and above all the extinction of huge numbers of animal and plant species, many of which being unidentified.

Founders of empires are usually better at conquering than they are at helping the populations that they conquer. Our industrial empire has not escaped this rule. As in the past, our attitude has not just been imperial; it has also been enormously reckless. Most Development to which we have attributed so many virtues has no future.

If they could see us today, Bacon, Kepler, Hobbes, Torricelli, Pascal, Huygens, Locke, Newton and all the other great thinkers and philosophers who did so much to lead us into the Enlightenment, would turn in their graves. We ignore the wisdom that they associated with the development of humanity. We are stuck on the path of heedless Progress by our own choice.

At the beginning of the eighteenth century, Denis Diderot, who published the first encyclopedia, explained that, "There are three principal means of acquiring knowledge available to us: observation of nature, reflection, and experimentation. Observation collects facts; reflection combines them; experimentation verifies the result of that combination. Our observation of nature must be diligent, our reflection profound, and our experiments exact."[46] We have heeded his words but only to enable ourselves to extract as much profit as possible, as quickly as possible, from what we are doing. As ego-systemization demands. Our reflection does not take into account the future.

Our faith in the race for Development is so deeply rooted that it is difficult to see how we can keep our world from sliding into a state of chaos.

CHAPTER 20

Forbidden Growth

T he further our Development progresses, the more colossal the number of ergamines employed by all types of industry becomes. Even our freeways filled with millions of cars behave like an industry.

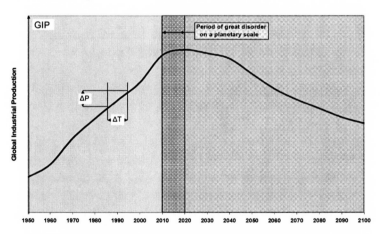

Global Industrial Production (GIP)

ΔT = change in time   ΔP = change in GIP

The graph shown here represents Global Industrial Production (GIP). Because the Industrial Wave is inseparable from the Energy Wave the curve of this graph mirrors the Global Energy Wave presented in the previous chapter.

Global Industrial Production has increased enormously since 1950. During this period, the increase of industrial production (ΔP) over time (ΔT) has been nearly permanent and can be expressed mathematically: $(\Delta P)/(\Delta T) > 0$.

Then, about the year 2010, the world will reach a historic turning point. The earth will no longer be able to provide enough energy to satisfy demand and the rate of increase of the Industrial Wave and the Energy Wave will slow down. Between 2010 and 2020 the world will feel the energy shortage as a "metabolic" deficiency as industrial growth gradually drops to zero: $(\Delta P)/(\Delta T) = 0$. The term "growth" will become obsolete. In some countries, it might even become forbidden, like it used to be in prehistoric times when new techniques, simple as they were, were perceived as threats to the precarious equilibrium of the tribe. After 2020, society will demand that development projects be sustainable.

Industrialized countries will need to adapt their societies to a *modus operandi*, which will become increasingly conservative energywise as time goes on. The adjustments that they make will impact all countries, including industrialized hydrocarbon producing countries, like Russia and Canada. Less "developed" countries possessing fossil fuel reserves will be strongly encouraged to give up their remaining energy resources to the great powers which lack them.

The period 2010-2020 will certainly be a time of industrial upheaval and disorder. But will this disorder really be disorder?

Since the beginning of the Industrial Era, human activity has been based on an increasing abundance of energy without taking into account that the use of these valuable resources creates conditions that are not necessarily sustainable. International commerce is an example of non-sustainability. A huge amount of the goods used by Western countries are currently made in Asia. Their production requires almost as much energy there as it would in the United States or Europe so it really makes little difference where they are manufactured. However, transporting these goods from Asia to the consumers requires phenomenal amounts of fuel. The same is true for food. Most of the items on the menu of a typical New Yorker, Londoner or Parisian have traveled thousands of miles mostly by plane to reach them.

Industrial development has created disorder in nature. Even if we have not deliberately created disorder, we must admit that almost all our activities result in it. We create disorder in agriculture when we feed crops with artificial fertilizers and treat them with herbicides, fungicides and insecticides. We also know what will happen to the insects, birds and marine creatures that eventually ingest them. We create disorder when we emit fossil carbon into the atmosphere. We create disorder when we change the natural state of minerals. Bauxite, an aluminum mineral composed of aluminum oxide (AL_2O_3) together with silica and iron oxides, is a natural compound. Not only do we extract aluminum from it, we then combine the aluminum with other metals to make alloys that nature does not create by itself.

Nature and Man do not have the same sense of order. Nature, as varied as it is, is structured. From a human point of view, what we call "order" in the agricultural, industrial or chemical domain is almost always disorder in nature. Agriculture is our prime disorganizer; by destroying biotic diversity, it ruptures the equilibrium of the intricately arranged living world. Our ego-systems are generally founded on principles in direct conflict with the equilibrium, and thus sustainability, of the natural world.

The coming energy shortage will force us to curb our propensity to create disorder. Of course, business will not necessarily see it in a positive light. The World Trade Organization who is contributing heavily to the disorder will rapidly be affected. This new, wiser attitude forced on us by nature will upset what is commonly known as "the order of things."

Even before the Industrial Wave crests, international commerce will have changed a great deal. Production centers will have been relocated. Populations too will have reconsidered their geographic locations. Major population concentrations far from agricultural production centers, and dependent on energy fuels, will be particularly affected. Some parts of the earth will experience the effects of global warming more severely than others. With little water, no local agriculture, the increasingly difficulty to obtain food and just a few tourists, Las Vegas is likely to become another Nevada ghost town. Built in a semi-desert climate and essentially conceived to commercialize play, it is in itself a monument to man's irresponsibility.

The stakes are extremely high. Industrial society has taken an enormous risk by not slowing down its Development. By continuing to advance in this insane fashion, it is now playing Russian roulette with the very existence of *Homo sapiens.*

Western society is built on the concept of consumerism and growth and cannot survive on any other terms. We will need to rethink its very foundations when the economic model that has been its basis for more than two centuries will no longer be able to maintain it.

Is our society capable of such self-analysis or is it instead condemned to decline as have all previous empires? It certainly seems that industrialized countries, which know no other means of stability than growth, will be unable to avoid a dreadful fate.

In Paris in January 2006, Dominique de Villepin was still betting on an economic recovery to improve his results as Prime Minister. His Finance Minister announced the expectation of "a gain of 2 to 2.5%" for the French Gross Domestic Product (GDP) for the year. At the same time, the opposition party, which was the Socialist Party, took the view that there was still insufficient economic growth to ensure industrial stability and therefore jobs. Independently, the French *Institut National de la Statistique et des Études Économiques* (INSEE) confirmed an increase of GDP thanks to business investment and household consumption. Some economic experts commented that French purchasing power for the coming years was likely to increase.

These statements show how dependent the health of France's economy is on industrial growth. Whether left or right wing, the French political parties have no other solution for keeping their society in good health than to "bet" on economic growth. This political orientation is not new. It is actually one of the rare constants of every French government since 1945.

The quest for "growth" is not peculiar to France. It is a general policy worldwide. Even the communist society of USSR understood the industrial order in terms of production growth. According to Marxist doctrine, industry and agriculture were supposed to produce so much that they could ensure work for everyone and there would be enough consumable goods to share. The Communist system was based as much on a powerful production-consumption cycle as it was on the equitable distribution of goods. Russian Communist society was just a mega ego-system with the Kremlin being a mega production planning center and the Russian people a mega consumer society. It is on these principles that the USSR functioned for seventy years. It is partly because the Socialist Union was unable to maintain its production-consumption cycle that it collapsed. Now Western countries face the end of their production-consumption system as well, although for different reasons.

All industrialized countries base their economic objectives on the assumption of inexhaustible resources. This very utopian attitude leads us to exhaust, in good conscience, all of the earth's valuable non-renewable natural reserves.

Stability through growth! This fine contradiction in terms alone might explain the sickness now eating at our society.

With this crisis looming on the horizon, it is high time that we checked on our Train of Progress. Is it still speeding up? Does its engine need a bit of a rest? Should not we check the rails or repair the coaches? Have the passengers been warned at of the dangers? Is there at least the chance of reaching a safe and peaceful destination? It seems that the passenger who, in my futurist vision, replied brusquely to the young man who had just boarded the Train, "You don't stop

Progress!" may have gotten it a bit wrong. In fact, our type of Progress will be stopped. This will not prevent some great visionary economist from continuing to proclaim that Western type society is still on the path of Progress. Man can only progress! It is even possible that to keep fuelling the engine, some will contemplate extreme solutions. Biofuel is already one.

The future of the rich nations essentially depends on the economic health of their industries. This is true in Europe, Japan, Taiwan, the Federation of Russia, Malaysia, South Africa, Indonesia, Australia, the United States, as well as China and India who are growing at explosive rates. All the more or less "developed" countries will be affected by the slowing down of Development.

What will happen to the United States that speeded up its ego-systematic Development the most? It is the USA that has coupled the most coaches to the Train of Progress, which now covers the world and maybe half of them carry the trademarks of American corporations. It is also the USA that has developed the most impressive militarized ego-systems which are capable of wiping out the human race in a matter of minutes. It is the United States that still ventures into new technological domains, consuming vast amounts of raw materials. It is thus logical that the United States should be expected to go the furthest on the Train of Progress. But this may be a very inhospitable place, unlike any place we have seen before and strange and unsafe. Perhaps the passengers of the Train will not even dare get off.

CHAPTER 21

Riding Progress

It was not until 1980 that I realized that our entire industrial system, our way of life, and our "civilization" were supported by an ephemeral wave, a wave that becomes more and more ephemeral as it accelerates through our Development. Before then, I never could have imagined how Man, with all his History, his Revolutions, the backing of his Institutions and Universities, could entrust his future to an ephemeral force. Every time I tried to discuss this question with others I did not get very far. My claims that oil would become scarce in the near future were almost invariably met with disbelief. "But, Pierre," they said, "We will find something else."

No civilization has ever withstood the test of time, but no civilization has ever devoured time as voraciously as ours. The economic system that we have chosen has made us consider time as something to overcome rather than to appreciate. "Time is Money" is truly a characteristic of the Industrial Era of the 19th and 20th centuries and it continues to be so in the 21st century. We could slow down enough to see what is happening around us. We might even find a sustainable speed. But instead, we continue to accelerate and to develop a society that has absolute confidence in the merits of perpetual Development. Our unquestioning faith in the future of our society has become a religion and any skepticism about the "American Way" can be seen as heresy.

Contrary to what one might think, it is not hard to spot the ephemerality of the Industrial Wave that we are riding. It is easy to feel its presence in all industrial activities, large or small. A few years ago, I visited some abandoned gold and silver mines in the American West. These sites are reminders of the mad Development that consumes us. Some mines in Nevada and California led to the birth of amazingly dynamic towns, like Virginia City and Bodie; most, however, were much more modest. One of them was a silver mine where my wife's grandfather had been a manager. It is situated in the middle of the Nevada desert. The only indication of mining activity at this site was a hill of tailings and an historical marker. The sign commemorating the miners' endeavor reads:

FAIRVIEW
1905-1917

Discovery in 1905 of a rich silver float led to a boom that lasted through 1906 and 1907. A substantial town that boasted 27 saloons, hotels, banks, assay offices, a newspaper, post office and a miner's union hall came into being. By 1908, the boom had passed and production levelled out. During 1911, the Nevada Hills Mining Company began an era of profitable milling that lasted until 1917. Production amounted to 3.8 million dollars in silver values.

STATE HISTORICAL MARKER N°202
NEVADA STATE PARK SYSTEM
DAUGHTERS OF THE AMERICAN COLONISTS
RENO CHAPTER

All that remained of this brief and frenetic enterprise were some foundations of former dwellings and a little spring with a few patches of watercress growing around it.

The Fairview mine was short lived, to say the least. It was not unique in this respect. Since those days we have more than kept up the pace of those miners. In the 1970s I was involved in the construction of an offshore platform, so massive it dwarfed the Eiffel Tower. It was built to exploit not silver but natural gas in the North Sea. Although situated in Norwegian waters, the gas was to be exported to England. We had to install enormous compressors on the platform to compensate for the loss of natural pressure within the deposit during the extraction process. They had to maintain the gas under pressure to make it flow to the English shore. This industrial complex, built in some of the roughest waters of the North Sea, constituted an ego-system in itself. Despite the enormous size and cost, it was never designed to operate for more than about ten years which was the "life expectancy" of this Norwegian gas deposit. True to expectations, this huge equipment was decommissioned several decades ago.

These two ventures, the Fairview silver mine in Nevada and the Norwegian platform in the North Sea, are caricatures of the industrial venture. There is no difference between their objectives and those of developments now being carried out by industrialized societies worldwide. They all progress toward the total exhaustion of valuable natural resources. Gold mines, silver mines, copper and lead mines, gas deposits, sardine shoals, schools of tuna, virgin forests, all are fated to disappear.

Our unrestrained use of energy has led us to activities that we should never have dared to undertake. Our Development has reached a level far in excess of the earth's capacities. We act as if we are living on a planet one hundred times larger than earth, perhaps larger even than Jupiter or Saturn. We need to "come back down to Earth." The industrial course that we are pursuing is not only beyond the earth's capacities, but also beyond our own capabilities.

The use of energy has always been presented to us as a convenience and never as a danger when, in fact, our massive consumption of energy leads us to undertake material developments far too complex to be controlled. There is a popular tendency to trust in the managers of industry who, we assume, are capable of controlling the equipment that they use, but this trust is particularly misplaced. As I have mentioned before, there are currently 30,000 billion energy slaves keeping our global ego-system running. Experience has shown that we cannot control so colossal a force without making some serious mismanagement. Our multitudes of cars, airplanes and ships are all damaging our planet as much as our factories and mines. We are unable to lead the regiments of ergamines at our service without causing seriously destructive side-effects. We are destroying entire sections of the earth's biota. Our dear, blue planet is biologically incapable of withstanding our general attack on it.

It took James Lovelock[i] nearly forty years to convince the scientific community that the earth is a global ecosystem that is self-sustaining and self-regulating like any biological organism. This acknowledgement is known as the Amsterdam Declaration of 2001. In his book *The Revenge of Gaia* [47] Lovelock makes it clear that earth is capable of restoring its own equilibrium after disasters, natural or man-made, but at a far slower pace than the rate of destruction we are causing through our Development. Earth and Man do not operate on the same time scale. It will take the earth hundreds of thousands of years to repair the damage that we can cause in just a few centuries, even a few decades. And the adjustments that we are requiring of it will not necessarily be favorable to human beings.

We impose no limits on ourselves. Through our extravagance and our lack of judgment, our society has reached the point of madness, in the literal sense of the word. We only need to look at what is happening in the shipping industry to see that this madness is very real indeed. The number of cargo ships sailing the seas doubles every ten years. Fishing factory boats are becoming more and more numerous and sophisticated. Cruise liners are now the size of floating towns. Between

---

[i] James Lovelock is an independent English scientist who invented the electron capture detector that detects man-made chemicals. His detector was used to determine that pesticide residues were present in virtually all species on Earth and even in mothers' milk. He also used it to discover the man-made chlorofluorocarbons (CFCs) which were depleting the stratospheric ozone layer. James Lovelock is best known as author of the "Gaia hypothesis" named after Gaea, Greek goddess of Earth.

2006 and 2009, the number methane tankers transporting liquefied natural gas, maintained at a cryogenic temperature of -260°F, will increase from 180 to 300, and their individual capacity will increase from 140,000 m^3 to 220,000 m^3. Shipbuilding yards have never been as inundated with orders for colossal vessels as they are today. With its over-powerful machines, industrial society has reached a stage of massive over-development.

CHAPTER 22

Descent of the Industrial Wave

What will happen when we start to run out of the magic potion that fuels our Development? The United States will obviously be extremely affected. Although it has only 4.5% of the world's population, it consumes approximately 25% of the world's energy production. This figure is probably closer to 30% if the flood of ergamines fuelling its military forces scattered around the globe and the energy used by the Asian factories producing goods for the United States are included in the calculation. Americans will need to react vigorously if they want to avoid disaster. In this country, private or "free" enterprise is king. Making money through increased production maintains its course but, in the process, irreplaceable natural resources are exhausted to produce capital which has only an artificial value. When resources are gone, the capital will not be able to bring them back. The process only works one way. American society is in the hands of opportunists. Republicans and Democrats support more or less the same economical system that leads to a money culture.

At the crest of the Energy Wave, when there is no longer sufficient energy and raw materials to keep industry turning, the capital will lose its value. The Industrial Wave will begin to decline and capital will no longer produce dividends, it could even lose its value completely.

The US business world is made up of a multitude of ego-systems that are all inextricably interconnected. Together they form such a complex mega ego-system that no manager, politician, or economist could ever claim to operate it differently. To exacerbate the situation, the laws that protect the country's economic system discourage any attempt to slow down Progress.

Although people may criticize the managers of industry, they themselves are in reality at the heart of the mega ego-system. Besides the fact that they keep it functioning in practical terms, they are inextricably tied to the monstrous beast that is industrial society by two "umbilical cords," the consumer cycle and the stock market.

The consumer cycle is vital for business and fundamental to the economy of the country. Through a barrage of advertising, citizens are pushed to consume more and more. They are shown everywhere and almost all the time that what they own is old-fashioned, or even obsolete. Their psyches are targeted in every way until they feel that they can only define themselves by what they buy, "I shop therefore I am."

Caught up in the ever growing cycle of advertising → desire for possession → purchase → consumption → discarding, American citizens are urged to buy products, even if they are superfluous or actually useless, and then to consume or dispose of them in record time. This perpetual cycle of the throwaway society allows factories to keep producing and renewing their production. It is one of the most important principles of the consumer society of which the United States is the prototype. Constant need inculcated to the people is also a need of the industrial world. Madagascans, for example, have different needs than Westerners. They just seek to satisfy their hunger. In their struggle for food, they keep their dignity. In Madagascar, advertising barely exists.

The second cord tying Americans to the business world is the stock market. This constitutes one of the financial cornerstones of the country and largely explains its economic buoyancy. Even if two-thirds of total stock market wealth is held by only five percent of American stockholders, the rest of the population uses the stock market as the basis for its retirement, through 401 K and other plans. This overall investment in industrial development accelerates the Train of Progress. Through the stock market, the average American, even if he sometimes disapproves of their policies, indirectly supports the major corporations, McDonalds as well as General Motors, Wal-Mart as well as Boeing or Google, and fragmentation bomb-manufacturing as well as trout-farming.

Business and people are inseparable economic partners. Any serious problems experienced by one will have inevitable repercussions on the other. The energy shortage will have an economic impact on the two partners. Americans and free enterprise have long been joined for the better; they will need to face the worse.

How will the American people and their business world react to the energy crisis? How will the government itself react? Will it disassociate itself somewhat from the major corporations and finally give priority to the people? Will it nationalize certain essential activities, such as the generation and distribution of energy or water management to ensure that the whole population has access to the utilities that are vital to them? Or, will it instead sacrifice society on the altar of business and allow corporations to carry on with no other consideration than profitability?

It already seems paradoxical to speak of American society when it is run mainly by large corporations entangled in blind ego-systems. As Dominique Quessada puts it, "Under pressure from transnational companies, political power – in other words, the power of organizing society, administrative activity, actual governance and all political affairs – moves from the political to the economic. ... In this way, business becomes the only point of access to social issues."[48]

In the 1930s, Franklin D. Roosevelt dared to imagine a society of sharing, but the Second World War stifled the social impulse of the country. After 1944, the major corporations who had been working flat out to sustain the Allied armies on all fronts, gained much power and with it, *de facto*, the right to lead society. In the 1980s, through a policy of deregulation, Reagan definitively reduced the role of the individual to that of the servant of business. Recently, G.W. Bush has gone even further. His policy presents social services as a burden on society and he openly wishes to privatize every aspect of them. For the American extreme right the best policy is survival of the fittest economically. America has reverted to unrestrained capitalism.

When the energy crisis starts to be felt, the American people are likely to find themselves on their own. The two following examples support this theory.

The first concerns the health system. The American health system is profit-based. It is difficult to believe that its primary objective is to care for the American population when current prices paid by individuals for hospital care and surgical operations are five to eight times higher than in Europe. Like every other activity in the United States, the health system is ego-systemic. Illness is without doubt a renewable source of profit.

The second example concerns Louisiana. The experts who have analyzed the course of events following Hurricane Katrina in September 2005 have shown that there was no adequate federal plan laid out in advance to help those who might suffer from such an event. The hurricane was certainly exceptional, but it was not the first to hit the region with such force. The flooding was largely foreseeable but the facilities for pumping water were not themselves protected and so were rapidly put out of service. When the damage was done and thousands of homes were under water, it still took ten days for the first rescue teams to reach certain neighborhoods to check whether any people, dead or alive, remained trapped in the flooded areas. The oil companies, located just off the coast in the Gulf of Mexico, employ professional divers to work on their offshore platforms but, apparently, none of the diving companies were called on in the days following the hurricane to help rescue the people of New Orleans. They could only be mobilized by the corporations. Not the government.

Americans will be powerless when the Industrial Wave begins to descend. Spread out in suburbs far from their work-places, with few public transport systems, totally dependent on private industry for essential items, and fed by an agribusiness running basically on cheap energy, they will experience serious difficulties. When business begins to slow down, and when gasoline, natural gas, electricity, food and even water become difficult to obtain, the people will want to know the underlying causes for this situation, causes that their leaders have hidden from them, but it will be too late to react sensibly. With no guarantee of help around them, they will fear losing everything they have acquired, and potentially the means of surviving economically, or even in some cases, physically. At a loss for a solution, they will have to abandon the superfluous. They will have to do without anything non-essential; in other words, without all the useless products that they buy now.

Business will be trapped by the lack of energy to maintain production and the decline in consumption. Many companies will likely disappear.

Modern society is not prepared for the descent of the Industrial Wave. Industrialized nations are only designed to keep moving forwards. The capitalist system only allows for Development. Lack of Development does not bring Progress. It does not even maintain the *status quo*. Industrialized societies are built on unstable foundations. Deprived of energy, they will dissolve as surely as ice cubes in the freezer without electricity.

So would it not be time to place conductors on the Train of Progress? Conductors who could start to slow down society while ensuring some security for the people? But who are the conductors on whom Americans could count?

In the event of financial difficulties, the leaders of private enterprise will have only one solution available to them: to cut costs, which in most cases will mean to cut personnel even further. If their financial difficulties become insurmountable, they will close down. It will be foolish to count on them.

This leaves the leaders of the country. The government in Washington D.C. above all represents the business world and has virtually no means of helping society to pass the crest of the Industrial Wave with little damage. Ego-systems have no other role, nor even any other option, than to continue directing their activities towards profit. This is clearly shown by the extreme feebleness of Washington's response to climate change.

Too much capitalism kills capitalism. Any economic system that functions without limits will inevitably lead to excess, and this in the end will destroy it. The United States is nearing the breaking point.

The decline of American society will follow a more natural course than its Development which was artificial and excessive. The age of shortage will replace the age of excess. The materialistic society to which the American people have become accustomed promotes individualism. It will not be easy for the population to replace individualism and their materialistic society with a sense of solidarity.

European and Japanese societies are theoretically better prepared to deal with the decline; or rather, to deal with it less badly. In "Old Europe," many of the reins of the ego-systems are still in the hands of government, which has some power to intervene when necessary. The population is more concentrated in mixed-use urban areas. There are national transport networks in operation. Towns still have some autonomy over their food supply because agribusiness has not totally taken over food production. The political parties still have a social role and support systems are already in place for people in need.

Most of the South American and African societies will not require a huge effort to return to a recent past when their people had a more sustainable way of life. Of course, they will obviously be forced to hand over their remaining valuable natural resources to Western ego-systems.

If history repeats itself, as it sometimes does, a new sage may appear on the scene like Confucius or Buddha, or more recently Mahatma Gandhi, Mikhail Gorbachev or Nelson Mandela, to help us out of the mire. Our trust in the future will be the most delicate part of the rescue because we have been seriously deceived by those who failed to help us prepare for the descent of the wave of ease. To find options, "developed" countries can always turn to the people who have remained wise, in particular those who have been so generously called "under-developed" by the West over centuries of Progress.

Our faith in Development will certainly diminish. We must hope, but it is only a hope, that the aspirations to achieve sustainable living will soon become again a real human value. Otherwise, the world will just go from crash to crash until Man has cleared the earth of everything potentially of value.

By plundering natural resources to exhaustion and by destroying the equilibrium of our habitat, we are not just treating our planet in a cavalier fashion, we are robbing life from future generations. Our way of life is not just unsustainable; it is immoral.

CHAPTER 23

Peak of Man's Irresponsibility

D uring their long evolution our *Homo sapiens* predecessors experienced the true difficulties of existence. If they had not been profoundly aware of their environment, they would never have been able to make the journey that has led to us, the dashing *Homo sapiens sapiens* of the 21st century. During their long journey through time, they saw several "cousins" disappear. The last of these, *Homo sapiens neanderthalis*, their "closest cousin" during 600,000 years, disappeared less than 25,000 years ago. Our existence today is truly astonishing. Considering the large number of predators that prehistoric Man had to outwit merely to survive, and the small number of children that the women could bear during their short life span, the survival of the human race was far from assured. The fact that only a single species of the *Homo sapiens* genus has survived shows how problematic, perhaps even unexpected, this survival is in terms of probability.

Apparently, the difficult times experienced by the thousands of generations that preceded us have been erased from our collective memory. Sometimes we erased them deliberately and attributed a sacred origin to the creation of Man. Yet, they are important if we are to understand how irresponsible our present behavior is.

During my short visit to the savanna in Chad, I learned that predation is constant. It is part of nature's way of maintaining life. In nature, very few animals, and very few men too, expect to live a full life span. One day or another they will fall to the continual cycle of predation. We have removed ourselves from the hazards of this cycle. We now give up our bodies to doctors instead of predators and, moreover, exterminate any species presenting the slightest physical threat to us. But we go beyond mere protection of ourselves and destroy anything that may interfere with our wellbeing. We are making the earth into the Earth of Man, our global ego-system. Super-protected, super-pampered, we are convinced that the future is ours and that we are too intelligent to have gotten things wrong.

We believe Progress to be well founded, when in fact it goes against nature, against our own future. Society's greatest institutions drive us to adopt this reprehensible behavior. Our schools prepare us to carry it out logically and scientifically. Our businesses enable us to achieve it economically. Our national institutions provide the framework for it legally.

The Industrial Revolution is often considered to be a real achievement of humanity – this is certainly how it is presented in most Western schools. But future generations may not be so generous. Even today some peoples of the world do not view it in a positive light. The Development based on technology has never been properly thought through. Societies that have accepted the industrial rise have, *de facto*, accepted man's exploitation *ad infinitum* of the planet.

Absorbed by our ego-systems, we have forgotten that we are living on a planet that has its own natural systems and laws. Although they have been disrupted in the past by catastrophic physical phenomena such as extensive volcanic eruptions, meteorite crashes, and successive warming and cooling periods, planet Earth has always been able to restore a tissue of life. Of all the species that have ever existed on earth, probably more than 99% are extinct. "The longest lived genus having inhabited the earth [has not stayed on it] more than five per cent of life history (Signor, 1994)."[49] The extinction of species is not something exceptional on earth. The new and brutal attack that our Development is inflicting on the earth is leading to an ecological disaster as severe as the earth has known since life began. Are we going to wake up?

Our carelessness towards life in general is far more worrisome than the energy crisis itself. The systematic plundering of fossil fuels is now a fact. Not content just to deplete all the fuel stocks, we are also using them to deplete other valuable resources. The exhaustion of many mineral substances is already well advanced. In January 2005, the United States Geological Survey (USGS), in charge of tracking the terrestrial reserves of exploited or exploitable mineral products, recorded that 25 of the 66 listed non-fuel minerals have estimated reserves of less than 60 years. Tin, lead and copper are amongst the 25.[50] I should add that the easiest reserves to exploit have already been depleted and that the exploitation of the remaining ones will require more and more energy as time goes on. Unless we wake up, we will carry on until we have totally exhausted all the precious reserves accessible to us. We will keep justifying our actions with "noble" reasons.

Blindness to the limits that life on earth can accept is characteristic of our modern society. It is becoming harder and harder to justify our Development. We act as if we were no longer responsible for our actions. If not forced to change our course by external factors, it is highly unlikely that we would ever do so. Just as some battles only came to an end for lack of soldiers, the general pillage of earth's resources can probably only be slowed down by the lack of energy. For this reason, the imminent energy crisis will end up being providential. It will set a limit on the irresponsible attitude that we have adopted over the past two centuries in our pursuit of Progress.

The peak of man's irresponsibility and the peak of energy production are coinciding fortuitously. Nature is reminding us, as it did before we embarked on our glorious industrial adventure, that we must use more wisdom as we pursue our course as *Homo sapiens*. There is a chance that nature will come to the rescue of the human race through the finiteness of its energy resources. Without this ultimate check, we might have systematically dredged the bottoms of the seas, pulverized all the limestone into concrete, filled our valleys with waste, digitalized the growth of plants, cybernetically organized our own conduct... Without even noticing it, we might have scientifically organized chaos.

Human disaster on a global scale clearly remains a distinct possibility. Few empires have been able to manage a sensible decline and it is unlikely that we will resign ourselves to passing the peak of Progress without a struggle. Some nations will not abandon the quest for supremacy to which industry has accustomed them. They will continue to follow their opportunistic policies and will not limit their exploitation of the globe. The current conduct of the United States in the Middle East gives a glimpse of the battles that could ensue when energy problems really start to kick in.

The irresponsibility of industrial society cannot be replaced overnight with a philosophy of great human wisdom. It would be utopian to think that. Moreover, it is highly likely that the earth itself, whose equilibrium is already in jeopardy due to climate change and the numerous attacks that we are inflicting on it, will not be able to satisfy our insatiability. It will not even be able to feed us all. Whether we admit it or not, our planet is already forcing us to adopt a more sustainable way of life. We have entered a period of crisis on a global scale, even if many of us deny this fact or merely pay it lip-service.

PART IV

HUMANITY PLAYS WITH FIRE

CHAPTER 24

Immature Man

In the 1970s, James Lovelock determined that the earth is a living being in that it is capable of maintaining its own physicochemical equilibrium. Today, if we have a better idea of how the human body maintains a balance, we still are not close to understanding how our planet does so. Yet Lovelock's discovery is capital and it is viewed by many scientists as important as Darwin's revelation about evolution.

Balance exists throughout nature and in fact it is on this balance that our own existence most depends. The interactions between the earth's elements determine the state of our planet at any given second. If we accept this assumption regarding the earth's equilibrium, we must also accept that there are limits to the extent to which it can be altered before we threaten life. The destruction of the ozone layer over the poles by the emission of chlorofluorocarbons is an example of the damage we can cause on earth.

This acknowledgment is only the first small step in understanding our planet. The most difficult part remains to be achieved. We have always taken completely for granted all the possibilities which the earth offers us. We have never considered that it might itself require certain conditions in order to remain as it is. We assume that it can indulge our whims and mend the damage caused by our blunders. We know that it can spew fire from volcanoes and be shaken by violent earth-quakes, but we have not acknowledged that it might lose the equilibrium on which we depend. Still less have we considered that we need to understand it.

In short, we are behaving immaturely. It is time that we grew up because it is now very possible that Mother Earth could suffer irreversible damage from the pressure that her billions of children are placing on her. Particularly the billion in "developed" countries whose way of life is so totally unsustainable.

In 1765, the military doctors of Louis XV, King of France, published a dictionary of health[51] with his "approval and privilege." The following passage concerns the benefits of mercury as a medical treatment.

> The Ancients believed that mercury was a poison .... We are now freed from that error & it is more commonly used to treat illnesses. ...
>
> Mercury has the virtue of opening the pores & the glands, & of removing obstructions from those parts; this is why, in tumors of the glands, in scirrhus of the spleen, mesentery & liver, in ganglions & scrofula, it is beneficially used ... for, as all these illnesses are derived from a thick & viscous lymph, they require a powerful medicine to loosen it: nothing succeeds better in this than mercury, owing to its liquidity & weightiness .... Bleedings and purgatives should always be administered beforehand ...
>
> The mercury preparations which are most commonly used are red precipitate, white precipitate & yellow precipitate, *athiops mineralis*, factitious cinnabar, corrosive sublimate, soft mercury & mercurial panacea. ...
>
> The effect of mercury, when it is taken internally by mouth, or when it permeates through the pores of the skin, is to cause perspiration; & when it is amassed in a certain quantity, it stimulates an abundant flow of thick & fetid saliva, accompanied by pain, & swelling in the mouth. This is called *salivation* ...
>
> [Fumigation is the] most common means of inducing *salivation*, but it is also the most dangerous method which

has been invented as a cure ... for besides the pain & the considerable weakening that is experienced, the teeth also start to chatter violently and the nerves begin to cause trembling and convulsions ...

Today we know about the dangerous effects of mercury; it is again considered a poison in most applications. But our knowledge of the earth is no better than that of the human body for the doctors of Louis XV and yet our scientific pretensions are just as great. If we decide to right our wrongs without understanding how the equilibrium of life on earth is maintained, our treatments could be as perilous for it as the "mercurial panacea" was for patients in 18th century France.

CHAPTER 25

Worrisome Skies

We know that the atmosphere is an essential part of our environment; without its oxygen life would be quite different on earth. What we are not necessarily aware of is that it contains other gases, such as carbon dioxide (CO_2) and methane (CH_4), that are just as important for life as oxygen. In conjunction with water vapor, they create a greenhouse effect that maintains the average temperature of our planet at around 60°F. Without these gases, the average surface temperature of the earth would only be around zero °F, which would not have enticed our *Homo sapiens* ancestors out of their icy caves very often, if they had even managed to get that far in the first place.

The surface of the earth and the atmosphere are constantly exchanging greenhouse gases. Scientists are studying the impact of these gases on the greenhouse effect by measuring the variation of carbon concentration in the atmosphere. During the 500,000 years that preceded the Industrial Era, they have found that it varied between 380 and 590 (Gt)[i] over the course of very long cycles of around 100,000 years.

---

[i] A gigaton (Gt) of carbon is equivalent to 1 billion tons, or 10^9 tons.

Since carbon exists in nearly everything on earth, from the rocks to all forms of life, the processes of carbon exchange are very complex. I have simplified them into two types.

The first is emission. It is one-way; carbon leaves the surface of the earth to enrich its atmosphere. The second type, which will be discussed in the next chapter, is two-way as it involves the biochemical exchange of carbon between the atmosphere and the surface of the earth.

Before the Industrial Era, over a year's time, these two types of exchange were in equilibrium; the total amount of carbon that enriched the atmosphere was balanced by an equal net amount of carbon returning to the land and sea through biochemical exchanges. This equilibrium between emissions and returns stabilized the storage of carbon in the atmosphere.

At that time, natural phenomena such as forest fires, natural gases released from deposits in the ground and volcanic eruptions were the main sources of the one-way emissions. Anthropogenic carbon emissions represented a smaller source.

Today, mainly due to industrial activities, anthropogenic carbon emissions have increased tremendously, destroying the equilibrium of the carbon exchange between the earth and its atmosphere. I estimate that before 1750, annual carbon emissions averaged 5 Gt/yr, and that today they average 14 Gt/yr. They have been multiplied by almost three since our ego-systems began to take over the planet. The atmosphere is no longer a storehouse for carbon; it has become a dumping place for innumerable industrial gases that enormously magnify the greenhouse effect.

The amount of carbon released into the atmosphere greatly exceeds the ability of the ocean and land to reabsorb it. Each year more carbon is added to the atmosphere. The current rate is 3.5 Gt per year. From 1955 to 2006, the amount of carbon stored in the atmosphere increased by more than 20%. In 2006, it reached the concentration of 800 Gt. This is 210 Gt beyond the 590 Gt maximum of the past 500 millenniums or, to put it in other terms, "the excess of 200,000,000,000 tons of carbon that has been warehoused in the sky equals more than 40,000 times the weight of the pyramid of Cheops."[52]

Through our ill-considered Development, we have interfered with the atmosphere's role of controlling the earth's temperature. And we have not yet reached the peak of our carbon emissions; if over the course of 21st century we were to consume all available fossil fuels as it is assumed in the energy scenario exposed in previous chapters, the additional quantity of carbon that would be discharged into the atmosphere would be more than twice the amount of our carbon emissions of carbon in the 20th century. One of the reasons for this increase is that coal, which will be burned extensively in the future, emits 20% more carbon dioxide than oil, and 33% more than natural gas, for the same energy output. Another reason is the expansion of industrial activities that generate large quantities of greenhouse gases. Two of the biggest are mass deforestation and cement production. The enormous quantity of biomass burned in the deforestation of the equatorial zones of South America, Africa and Asia is producing a huge amount of carbon dioxide. Cement production also liberates carbon dioxide during the process of limestone decarbonation. China's industry is expanding so rapidly that in 2007, this country alone was responsible for nearly half of worldwide cement production.

It seems that it will be impossible to prevent the earth from warming up over several centuries. Even an immediate halt of greenhouse gas emissions may not enable us to avoid a global disaster. Yet this alarming situation has not persuaded the leaders of the most polluting countries to change their energy policies. Certainly not the American, as Naomi Klein emphatically says, "The Bush Administration, still roadblocking firm caps on emissions, wants to let the market solve the crisis. 'We are on the threshold of dramatic technological breakthroughs,' Bush assured the world last January [2007], adding, 'We'll leave it to the market to decide the mix of fuels that most effectively meet this goal.' "[53]

According to a study presented in January 2007 by the US Department of Energy, approximately 160 coal-fired electrical power plants are scheduled to be built in the next decade in United States. China and India have equally "ambitious" construction programs for coal-fired electrical power plants. Of all the types of power plants, these are the biggest producers of carbon dioxide.

In the face of such arrogance, it is hard to deny the irresponsibility of human society.

CHAPTER 26

Global Imbalance

E xcessive one-way carbon emissions have not only upset the system of climate regulation, they have also altered the two-way biochemical exchange of carbon between the earth and the atmosphere and, in particular, the recycling of carbon on the continents and in the oceans. This second phenomenon is just as worrisome as the first, yet it is not often mentioned.

The carbon that returns to land from the atmosphere maintains the land biota through the natural process of photosynthesis fueled by sunlight. During the day, as plants absorb carbon dioxide, carbon atoms are freed of their bonds to oxygen, enabling plants to produce the complex carbohydrates that are the building blocks of life. Although plants emit carbon dioxide during the night, overall they capture more carbon dioxide from the atmosphere than they emit. In this manner, carbon coming back from the atmosphere sows life on the continents – "today's smoke stack emissions from China become tomorrow's flowers in Vermont."

In addition to sowing life on land, carbon returning from the atmosphere also maintains life in the seas. It is even probably the means by which life began on our planet.

How carbon contained into the atmosphere returns to the oceans is a little complicated. Carbon dioxide enters the surface water by diffusion. Then, some of it is taken up by the marine flora concentrated along the continental shelves through photosynthesis. The rest dissolves and enters a cycle known as the dissolution-evaporation cycle that takes place in the surface water. Because the solubility of carbon dioxide increases in cold water, marine currents, acting like giant conveyor belts, load themselves with dissolved carbon when they surface around the poles and carry it to the deepest reaches of the oceans all around the world. When the currents resurface in the warm waters of the tropical regions, carbon dioxide is released into the atmosphere by evaporation.

Each year, the natural two-way biochemical-exchange moves around 200 Gt of carbon back and forth between the sky and the surface of the earth. The exchange is not exactly equal in each direction because the land and sea absorb more carbon than they emit. Prior to the Industrial Era, the average annual net mass of carbon in the atmosphere that was recaptured on land and in the sea was probably about 5 Gt and, as seen before, was equal to the emission. At 10 Gt/yr, today it is double that amount and, as surprisingly it may seem, we are a long way from understanding what happens to the extra 5 Gt. Many scientists admit that they cannot account for it globally and that some carbon seems to be "missing."

On the continents, the quantity of carbon that can be absorbed depends on the quantity of biomass. Since the beginning of the Industrial Era, land biomass may have decreased by more than 10% as urban areas and the general infrastructure of our ego-systems take over green spaces. The increase in world-wide production of food, fiber and now biofuels is converting zones of natural vegetation into agricultural land that, in general, has a smaller and less varied biomass. In addition, the tens of thousands of square miles of vegetation that are disappearing each year on land as a result of climate change and the advance of the deserts is reducing the amount of flora available to absorb carbon from the atmosphere.

If this "missing" carbon cannot be accounted for on land, it seems logical to look to the oceans. In principle, the diffusion of carbon dioxide in the surface waters of the oceans is proportional to its concentration in the air. Since 1750, this concentration has increased about 35%. So, the oceans seem to be able to reabsorb a larger amount of carbon than it is necessary for the production of phytoplankton. But, in fact, the extra carbon is contributing to the acidification of the water. Too much carbon adversely affects life by affecting the construction of calcium carbonate skeletal material of unicellular plants and animals, corals, mollusks and others. Acidification comes in addition to the rise in temperature of the oceans.

Contrary to what one might expect, the growth rate of phytoplankton around the world decreases in warm waters. Global warming could very likely limit even further phytoplankton production as the water temperature of the oceans rises. This might even be the most disastrous side-effect of our human activities. Because of its mass, marine flora is a huge consumer of carbon. The world cannot manage without this marvelous natural carbon sink that feeds the marine fauna. Unicellular phytoplankton forms the base of the food chain sustaining sponges, copepods, molluscs and others. Higher up the food chain come all the animals that make up the web of marine life: jellies, octopuses, fish, whales ... and on to polar bears.

Human activities have consequences just as serious for the marine flora as for the land flora. Recent assessments of the state of the marine flora are very disturbing. The NASA satellite data published in *Nature* in December 2006 showed a rapid increase of disappearance of marine flora in large zones of the oceans.

It is difficult to predict how the phenomena of diffusion, photosynthesis and dissolution-evaporation of carbon in the ocean will evolve. There is a strong possibility that marine currents will be altered by the melting of the Arctic ice cap, which would affect the dissolution-evaporation process of carbon in the ocean. But it is impossible to predict whether this change on a planetary scale will have a favorable or unfavorable impact on the marine carbon sink.

It is time that we become concerned about the fact that a significant amount of the carbon that we have extracted from fossil fuel deposits buried in the earth's crust and then burned is returning from the atmosphere to the land and sea. This phenomenon might be as serious as the greenhouse effect but it has not really been factored into the predictions.

Meanwhile we try to figure out where all the anthropogenic carbon coming back from the atmosphere is settling, the Train of Progress continues to spew out more and more smoke. Instead of developing our ego-systems any further, we urgently need to recognize the adverse effects that our Development has already had. This is what university researchers should be focusing on. Up till now the sums of money that they receive from industry mostly help the Train of Progress to move forward.

In 2007, the amount of money spent worldwide to study the effects of climate change attributed to human activities was in the order of 10 billion dollars. That same year, the total global revenue from the sale of gasoline and other fossil fuels exceeded 10,000 billion dollars. In other words, for each dollar spent to study the effect of global climate change, we spent 1,000 dollars producing more CO_2.

Humanity is literally playing with fire.

CHAPTER 27

The Deathblow

I t is likely that the energy shortage will take us to the limits
of what is humanly possible. We will turn to the other
sources of carbon-based fuel that have been relatively spared
until now.

The first victims of our addiction to energy could well be
what remains of the forests. Timber is of course an excellent
source of energy for heating and cooking but, as Western
Europe discovered in World War II when it was deprived of
oil, it can also fuel motor vehicles that are equipped with
systems to convert wood into gases.

Two other sources of carbon-based fuels are still almost
intact. These are kerogens and methane clathrates.

Kerogens are chemical compounds which derive from
the decomposition of organic matter. Their molecular formulae
are infinitely varied, ranging from very simple forms to
extremely complex organic macromolecules. They often occur
in the sedimentary layers of the earth. If the sedimentary rocks
containing kerogens are surrounded by watertight geological
formations kerogens form deposits that may eventually become petroleum or natural gas fields.

The mass of kerogens existing in the ground could be
one thousand times greater than that of the deposits of classic
fossil fuels. Some scientists envisage artificially aging natural

kerogens deposits to accelerate the process of fossilization so that petroleum fuels can be obtained rapidly but they are certainly not assessing the impact that such a development might have. Why not artificially age the entire earth the better to rob it of its riches?

Methane clathrates, more commonly called methane hydrates, CH_4 $6(H_2O)$, are made of methane (CH_4) and water. They constitute another immense stock of fossil fuel. Natural hydrate deposits contain many times more hydrocarbons than all worldwide oil and gas fields discovered and yet to be discovered. They are present in enormous quantities in the sea along the continental shelf, at depths of 1600 ft (500 meters) or more. They are also present in the Polar Regions, beneath the permafrost. They seem to form when natural gas or kerogens are saturated with water and maintained under certain conditions of pressure and temperature in the sea or under the earth's crust.

Until now, the process of extracting these hydrates has always required more energy than these fuels could themselves provide. We must hope that their use will never be efficient energy-wise because they would release enormous amounts of carbon dioxide and rapidly transform the atmosphere into a huge electric blanket turned on high. Yet this risk in no way deters the oil companies and research institutes, particularly in Japan, from considering this source of hydrocarbons as a substitute for natural gas.

With the consumption of our last forests, kerogens and methane hydrates we have the power to give the deathblow to Mother Earth.

PART V

VIA SAPIENS

CHAPTER 28

Existential Questions

T he questions that I ask myself about our irresponsibility towards the future are becoming increasingly "awkward." Given that I have spent my whole life promoting technology, I find them particularly unsettling.

What troubles me most is that we, in the Western world, seem to have virtually no doubts about the results of our undertakings. We seem to have no fundamental reservations about entrusting our future to industrial society. We are convinced that we belong to a society of Progress.

Of course there are many people who are against some industrial ventures and who express themselves strongly when necessary. Concerned citizens strive, often with real success, to preserve that which can still be preserved: the California coast, the virgin forests in Oregon, the Alaskan tundra, the Austrian Alps or the Australian coral reefs. Generally, however, Westerners accept the type of society that they have made for themselves. But, even if they would like to change certain aspects of their society, they do not necessarily wish to put the Train of Progress into reverse. Besides, such a wish could never be realized because the Train is designed to only move forward. With no brakes!

Overall, at present, there does not seem to be enough social concern in countries that have chosen the industrial way to foment any fundamental change. On the contrary, the industrialized world is convinced that it is "progressing." More and more countries are adopting our Western type of Development and the latest countries to board the Train, those of South-East Asia, are among the most dynamic.

With so much of the world now in the race for Progress, the time has come to ask ourselves some fundamental questions. Can we really no longer do without hummers, super jets, gourmet food, granite counters, bubbling Jacuzzis, giant flat screen TVs, leaf blowers and other superfluous acquisitions? Are we willing to compromise the physical existence of future generations so that we can today enjoy to the limit the luxury in which we have immersed ourselves? Will modern society carry on with the same dogged determination as the Forty-niners in California and the natural gas explorers in the North Sea to extract every last ounce of the rich deposits they found? Will we not see any drawbacks to depleting fossil fuels, minerals, aquifers, forests, rivers and, at the same time, wiping out wild flora and fauna?

I fear that we will answer "yes" to all of these questions. The great majority of us will just keep going down the path that we are on today. If we had come from another planet and had been forced to pillage the earth in order to survive, we would not have acted any differently.

Our politicians cannot escape our "enthusiasm." Though the art of politics consists of planning for the future, we do not let the politicians do so. In "developed" countries they know that we expect them to paint the sky blue and so, during their campaigns, they paint it blue. Once elected, we want them to satisfy our immediate desires and so they make admirable efforts to enable us to sate our insatiable "needs." For their part, our rush for consumption is the most effective way to raise the economic indices that ensure the success of their policies. Few of us could really see ourselves electing killjoys who promise only restrictions in their attempt to achieve a so-called sustainable way of life. Why would we content ourselves with less when we can have more? This simple question summarizes the advertising slogans that hound us everywhere; those that work best, in fact.

Since most of us do not really want the Train to slow down, we should ask ourselves if we are still able to think freely. Have we been indoctrinated? Has industrialized society inculcated in us such a strong faith in Progress that we do not even feel the need to check if what we are doing is just and in our best interest?

In the end, we need to understand how science, philosophy, history, religion and cultural traditions, for which we have such respect, have contributed to our present course and why they have not given us the wisdom to pursue Development in a sustainable way.

These are existential questions. They concern more the existence that we have chosen than our essence (from the Latin *esse* meaning "to be"), two concepts that have preoccupied philosophers for millennia.

Essentialists believe that Man's behaviour is above all determined by his *essence*, that is to say, all of his mental and physical capacities. According to Descartes, *essence* determines the *existence* of a being; *existence* is the realization of *essence*. Through his *essence*, Man can attain Reason. For Descartes, Reason includes Morality and Ethics.

Essentialists have known for a long time that human civilization is capable of excessive Development. The pyramids of Egypt, the Great Wall of China and the Roman Coliseum are vestiges from some of the civilizations that saw no limits to their power. But, at the beginning of the 20th century some philosophers, ever hopeful of a better world, expected that Industry would enable Man to organize society more wisely.

In reality, previous civilizations, as excessive as they may have been, never really threatened earth's equilibrium. Ours does. Our industrialized world represents the excess of excess. It is not just transforming the history of humanity; for the first time, because of the scale of its excess, it is jeopardizing the very balance of life on the entire planet.

At the end of the 19th century, Søren Kierkegaard, and more recently, Karl Jaspers, Jean-Paul Sartre and Simone de Beauvoir, to name but four, examined *existence* more independently. Twenty two century after Aristotle, Sartre reiterated that "*existence* precedes *essence*." In other words, we cannot define what it is to be human since our very being is defined through our own *existence*, by what we make of ourselves (of our *essence*). Individuals have far more freedom of action than the *essentialists* chose to envision.

These considerations should invite caution; we could be trapped in a cyclical way of thinking: by imagining that we possess Reason, we believe that what we are doing is reasonable. In reality, by using Reason, we have created unreasonable situations for ourselves. The cultural and intellectual baggage that we have acquired over several centuries, especially during the "Enlightenment," is inadequate in that it does not enable us to find a way of life that is sustainable. It seems that we even do not know exactly what we want to sustain.

How much longer are we going to proudly act like "the developed people" who know best? Not every path followed by Man necessarily leads to the depletion of nature, and the consequent imbalance of the earth. For instance, Buddhists consider themselves as part of nature and not its stewards.

We did not see ourselves as fatalists as we "developed" the world to such excess; we cannot be fatalists now. It would be just as dishonest to keep our heads in the sand as it would be immoral to say Man is headed towards an apocalyptic end.

CHAPTER 29

A Culture of Opportunism

Our lives begin to end the day we become
silent about things that matter

Martin Luther King Jr.[54]

A fter the Second World War, while Western Europe was busy recovering from its wounds, a profound dichotomy existed between philosophy that was taught in school and the way in which society behaved.

Philosophy was presented to students as an unparalleled art of thought in which Man explored the fundamental questions of existence. As René Descartes wrote, "I shall not say anything about Philosophy, but that, seeing that it has been cultivated for many centuries by the best minds that have ever lived, and that nevertheless no single thing is to be found in it which is not subject of dispute, and in consequence which is not dubious, I had not enough presumption to hope to fare better there than other men had done."[55] With philosophy, everything seemed open to discussion.

Outside the classrooms and the lecture halls, society just carried on at the mercy of events. Europe's main priority at the time was to develop its industry. Its chief concern was the immediate future. The common goal – Progress through technology – was not questioned. Development was highly valued, though it was only understood in material terms. Opening new mines, finding new construction materials, building modern factories, mechanizing manufacturing, testing new types of power generators, building new port facilities, and launching faster trains, longer-range airplanes, better armored tanks... There was never any thought given to the possibility of the limits of society, or the risk of exhausting the natural resources that lay behind the industrial movement.

It is true that European society placed much importance on social progress. It achieved significant results that are still today a model for the world. Even so, it never had the curiosity or the concern to consider its long-term future. In the classroom, philosophy was viewed as one of the foundations of the general culture; but outside school, when it came to driving the Train forward, philosophy was irrelevant.

Even tradition, several centuries old, was no brake to the rush for Development. Though each country tried to safeguard its own culture, the need for social and material progress always prevailed over cultural tradition. Some European countries, however, did not greet technological development so enthusiastically. The countries on the periphery of Western Europe, such as Iceland, Ireland or Greece, possibly because their small size did not allow them to foster any great ambitions, had time to examine the industrial path more carefully before taking it. Spain and Portugal, held back by autocratic governments, were also late in joining the movement.

In the more ambitious European countries, a career in industry was seen as a laudable aspiration, and a fine vocation. Following the destruction caused by World War II, the younger generation dedicated themselves to the reconstruction of their countries and, beyond that, to the Development of their societies. It was the general will, whether in Luxembourg, the Po Valley, Rotterdam, Liverpool or Frankfurt, that people "get back to work."

On an intellectual level, the post-war period was perhaps one of the emptiest in European history. Everybody wanted to enjoy life again. Few people questioned Progress. The development of nuclear energy in France, launched by General de Gaulle and his Prime Minister Pompidou, was overwhelmingly supported by industrial circles as well as even the most left-wing trade unions.

Despite the general acceptance of technological development, a few new schools of philosophy emerged here and there. Existentialism, in France, was one. Jean-Paul Sartre filled some of the intellectual void left by the war. His philosophy could not have been better timed. Existentialism spoke directly to the youth. It was theirs. However, apart from intellectual groups gathering in a few university towns and the Latin Quarter in Paris, Sartre's thoughts did not touch the general public. Sartre did, however, by reconsidering Man in the light of existence, help the young to determine more clearly what, in society, was just convention and what was not. With Sartre, they were able to indulge in a little philosophical reflection before embarking on their professional lives. Yet once on the Train, they only very rarely found the chance to revisit his philosophy.

In Western countries there were several important social movements that had a philosophical basis. The feminist movement was one of them. Feminists managed to improve the status of women. Through "The Second Sex"[i] and "The Feminine Mystique"[ii] Simone de Beauvoir in France and Betty Friedan in the USA were amongst those who convinced society of the need to review the position of women.

The Civil Rights movement to end racial segregation led by the Reverend Dr. Martin Luther King Junior was a very fundamental movement in the history of United States. The Civil Rights Act of 1964 and the Voting Rights Act of 1965 confirmed that all ethnic groups living on American territory

---

[i] Simone de Beauvoir, *Le Deuxième Sexe (The Second Sex)* (Paris: Gallimard, 1949). A detailed analysis of women's oppression and a tract of contemporary feminism. "Existence precedes essence," hence one is not born a woman, but society constructs one.

[ii] Betty Friedan, *The Feminine Mystique* (New York: W.W. Norton, 1963) Freidan thought that women were victims of a false belief that requires them to find identity in life only through their husbands and children.

would henceforth enjoy the same rights. This episode in American history is often seen in the Unites States as a social movement. From the point of view of the Afro-Americans it had also a much deeper objective. They were seeking access to a way of life that heretofore had been denied them. Their aspirations were philosophical, political and economic. The Civil Rights Act theoretically allowed them to become partners in the Development of society.

The hippie movement, in the 1960s, was another important philosophical movement in the post-war era in America. The hippies challenged the foundations of American society. They saw industrial society's lack of responsibility. They questioned established institutions and political and social orthodoxy. They criticized the values on which consumer society is based. Despite the fact that they never really redefined an alternative to the consumer society they hoped to tear down, their movement had a huge impact in the United States, particularly on the West Coast where a significant proportion of the population embraced the principle of zero economic growth. At around the same time, the American-Canadian writer and activist Jane Jacobs wrote the value of natural growth. But the big corporations proved far too powerful to accommodate principles that were very quickly dismissed as "utopian" by the establishment and these attempts of change were marginalized.

The fact that Western society did not really change direction does not mean that the period since 1945 has been uneventful in terms of social movements. On the contrary, they occurred on both sides of the Atlantic.

Europe experienced the "events of 1968," which were sparked by both students and workers. This civil unrest might have looked like a social revolution at times but, although people were challenging the status quo, they were not challenging the values of Development; they just wanted to benefit from it.

The communist system that Moscow imposed on Eastern Europe after World War II also had an effect on Western society. The Western European countries were forced to treat social issues with respect. In United States, on the other hand, it had a contrary effect after McCarthyism fostered a fear of it. By associating social progress with communism, it blocked social progress. The American society still suffers from this today.

These movements were all important, but they never demonstrated any real desire to examine the fundamental values of industrial society.

Today, the societies of Europe and North America, even if they increasingly differ in their treatment of social matters, are more than ever united on one point: they do not question their philosophical orientation. They just keep betting on Development and show little concern about its future. This is particularly true in the United States where production must always ensure immediate profit. The majority of Americans see the American way of life as the best in the world. Even "democracy," as far as they are concerned, is American.

American history books attach importance to the European revolutions of the end of the 18th century, as well as to the principles of liberty and equality associated with them. While these principles have been important throughout American history, over the last thirty years things have changed considerably. Society has become economistic; liberty is conceived more in terms of free economic competition than individual freedom. For many Americans, particularly the rich, Development is not just a right, it is a duty. Money is no longer just a value for exchange; it has become a sign of social superiority. Man and Society are no longer joined to further the common good; both of them try to take advantage of the other. The winner is money. Economic success is conspicuously displayed. Vast mansions reflect the respect given to money. Gigantic cars provide the status of grandeur.

But we are at the crest of the wave of "success." For Americans, Europeans and those who have followed them down the industrial path, the good times may be coming to an end. With the descent of the wave, consumer society will be forced to reassess itself. The imposition of Western culture on other countries, the general exploitation of "under-developed" populations, economic expansionism, promotion of the throwaway society, personal enrichment as a moral value, the exhaustion of irreplaceable natural resources, the quest for the superfluous at the expense of the environment, and finally the use of "democracy" as the spearhead of ego-systemization, are not philosophical values.

If I had to give a name to the fundamental motive that is guiding industrialized societies at the beginning of this third millennium, I would choose the word opportunism.

CHAPTER 30

Fundamentalism of Progress

I n the Dark Ages, the Christian Church justified the power of European kings, queens and princes over their subjects by blessing their power. According to the Church, God reigned over all things. It was not for lay Catholics to interpret the Holy Scriptures, to inquire about the laws of physics or to seek philosophical explanations of life. The Church was sole keeper of the divine word and religious beliefs had the value of philosophy. As a result, it was more a restrainer than a spiritual guide; more an enforcer than a counselor.

Almost every community on Earth, at some point in its history, has asked itself the delicate question of what role religion ought to have in society. The communities that have best succeeded in maintaining a harmony between religion and society are those that have been prepared to broach this question on a philosophical level. The Buddhists are among them.

This was not the case in European society. The Church of Rome refused to allow its followers to question the dogmas it imposed on them and to think independently. It jealously confined answers to the "wonder of the Lord's creation" and it never gave a satisfactory answer to those who sought to use Reason to gain some understanding of life and the world. Some wanted to understand what deprived mute, deaf and blind people of their senses. Others wanted to know more about the intriguing ballet of the stars in the sky. Were they of divine origin or made of matter?

Even priests were not supposed to ask fundamental questions about anything that touched on the sacred. And almost everything in society was sacred.

Through its intransigence, the Church lost credibility with the European scientific and philosophical elite in the 17th and 18th century. The great European thinkers of the Age of Reason tended to distance themselves from religion, sometimes quite radically. "Francis Bacon, counselor of King James I of England, insisted that all truth, even the most sacred doctrines of religion, must be subjected to the stringent critical methods of empirical science. ... [John Locke believed that in] the Age of Reason, and for the first time in human history ... men and women would be free, and, therefore, able to perceive the truth." Later, "Newton became almost obsessed with the desire to purge Christianity of Mythical doctrines."[56] Blaise Pascal, who finally chose to "bet on the existence of God," was no less severe in his criticism of the conduct of the Church.

Most of the revolutions that occurred in Europe during the 18th and 19th centuries made the separation of Church and State official. The Church's role was circumscribed to barely more than the saving of souls. Henceforth, Europeans would draw a distinction between society and religion: society concerned man; religion the soul.

Yet, if there was ever a real need for spiritual guidance, it was when the Industrial Revolution forged ahead. But the Church was not at the forefront. Faithful to its tradition of discouraging individuals to think on their own, the Church did not help the Europeans to reflect on the consequences of their actions as they proceeded with Development. Instead, it encouraged them to concentrate only on the egoistic matter of saving their souls. It did remind them not to act out of self-interest but to no avail. Rather than helping them in their quest for knowledge, the Church chose instead to hide behind a negativism concerning anything scientific or philosophical. It is true that some exceptional priests showed social responsibility by caring about intolerable working conditions and also that, in 1890, the Vatican supported labor unions but, if these initiatives helped the workers, they had no major influence on the industrial movement itself.

Of course, nowadays some Europeans remain ostensibly religious. Churches are still impressive. The funeral masses of dignitaries still draw other dignitaries. Christians regularly attend the church of their denomination, be it Catholic, Protestant or Orthodox; but aside from this demonstration of faith, European society is no longer guided by any great religious principle. Man reserves the right to make his own judgments and to use his mind in all matters. He is not limited in his endeavors by those who represent morality. As far as he is concerned, his activities, being directed towards the Progress of humanity, are by definition "moral." Man has become his own priest in all matters concerning society.

The Protestant Reformation tried hard to save Christianity which, during the 16th century, seemed adrift. It helped to make it more understandable by the people, to bring them as near to their God as anybody else. A shoemaker could be as close to his Lord as the Pope. However, in making religion more accessible, without any intermediary between a believer and his Lord, it gave Christians the freedom to justify their actions without the help of a priest. Bible in hand, Protestants could apply self-censorship and subscribe to unsustainable Development. It was God's will that the forest be cut, that workshops be built, that fish be caught. Justification by faith alone reinforced their trust in society's Progress. It led to the sanctification of work.

In the United States, there are many different churches. For the most part, they are Christian, even if many have fractured into different sects, as groups of individuals break away for ideological reasons. This sectarianism enables the individual to fulfill himself according to his own conscience. When the European immigrants first arrived in the Americas, they asked their religious representatives who came with them to sanctify the new lands so that they could be worked according to the will of God. Americans considered Development to be unique to Man and, therefore, "sacred."

So here we are. Convinced that we have found our path, we trust in the aims of our approach. We have gone from excessive fear about changing anything in our social behavior, which was the case in medieval time, to excessive freedom to undertake and develop everything. Convinced that man's quest for human Progress is of fundamental value, we do not think that it is necessary to analyze the future of Progress with any rigor. For two centuries, we have been racing from venture to venture, always confident of being able to resolve potential problems after the event.

We claim to pursue Development scientifically but, in reality, we do not act like scientists. While scientists, in line with their methodical approach, only accept the worth of that which can be proven, we do not analyze the final consequences of our activities. We are convinced that they can only be for the good of society and we base our undertakings more on faith than reason.

In the end, we are still people of faith! We have never really reached the Age of Reason that we claim to represent. Though we profess to be scientists, we act like fundamentalists. Our faith in the future is not based on any logical or material proof. We have become fundamentalists of our own Progress. Proselytizing our Development, denigrating other cultures, endlessly developing technologies, and imposing our ego-systems on the rest of the world, are just some of the dogmatic practices of Universal Progress in which we believe. Moreover, to strengthen our belief we entrust those in power with the mission of propagating this faith in Progress.

Unlike European society that has maintained a separation between the social and the religious, part of American society has melded fundamentalism of Progress and religious fundamentalism. The latter is often used by the country's Far Right to reinforce the former. The profane and the sacred are united to justify the excessive power of the princes of money. At times we do not seem very far from the days when the Church justified the power of princes of blood, and vice versa.

CHAPTER 31

Irresponsible Design

A minority of Americans do not accept the culture of un-restrained opportunism that has taken over their society nor do they want to see their country become increasingly imperialistic.

They are extremely concerned about the future of the United States. They cannot accept that wars are undertaken in their name just to satisfy the corporate world. They recognize the dangers posed by the federal government's subordination to the major corporations, whose sole aim is the pursuit of mega-profits, all too often by whatever means. They are also conscious of the irrationality of a way of life based on a system that the earth cannot sustain. All in all, they know that "the future will never be what it used to be" and are worried about what their society has in store for them in the long term.

Two opposing economic views are dividing American society. On the one hand, still very much in the minority, are those who recognize that the economic system, on which their society is based, is in jeopardy and they would like to change direction. On the other hand, are opportunists who look for immediate returns and are benefiting outrageously from unre-stricted free enterprise. They support the imperialist policy and, indirectly, govern the country. One might even say that the big corporations, fearing the worst, want to profit from the system right up to the end.

In reality, neither side is in a position to face the risky situation. Due to the infiltration of the corporate world in all branches of government, any desire for change remains theoretical. The American people are hostages of the industrialists, even of those who promote alleged environment alternatives such as so-called "alternative energies," as well as of opportunistic politicians who use the environment ideology to stay in power.

Since the Reagan era, America has become more nationalistic. This is not without danger for world peace. When a society is set on pursuing unethical objectives, it can become something quite other than the sum of individuals. Such a society can, little by little, lose its guiding values as Germany did it in the 1930s. Today, America has lost its moral path and is without any guiding philosophy.

It is difficult to foresee how the United States will change course even though some citizens would like to slow the pace and to reflect before proceeding "further." American society cannot wait. Nor can it undertake any rapid drastic shift without risking a major "fall-out." It is not unique in this respect; the European, Japanese and other industrialized countries cannot survive unless they too promote consumerism.

Trapped by our ego-systems, we have passed the tipping point and no longer have the ability to slow our momentum.

My own experience in the petrochemical industry in no way contradicts this terrible outcome. It was only after I had spent many years carrying out excessive industrial developments that I began to seriously question the foundations of "Western civilization." I know that we have let ourselves be carried away by our enthusiasm. The type of society in which we have placed such hope is not only unsustainable; it is as dangerous for the future of humanity as the worst imaginable war. Incapable of curbing our momentum, we have exceeded our intellectual capacities.

I would not be worried if immoderate and unsustainable Development was an isolated phenomenon promoted by only a few but this is not the case. In Western countries, Progress and Development are considered to be normal, just as it is considered normal for the young to head to the excellent universities of "knowledge": knowledge of how to exploit the last of the valuable and irreplaceable resources on Earth as rapidly and as legally as possible.

By failing to prioritize the values of our existence, we have lost control of our civilization. Future historians will view our "industrial epic" as insane.

No one can responsibly claim that Man, who dominates the world today, is the result of an Intelligent Design. He is embarked on an industrial odyssey that he cannot halt. He seems rather to be the fruit of an Irresponsible Design.

Where is Man Heading?

We know nothing truly about anything

Democritus, ca 400 BC

For a long time I believed in the future of Western society. Its Development seemed so rational that I did not even question it. I believed in Progress. It never occurred to me to doubt the sustainability of our society. I believed that we were on the right path. The Path! Without realizing it I was, like many of us, a fundamentalist of Progress. Man could only progress, and the faster he did so, and the greater his knowledge, the better his life would be. In all this, I was mistaken. The Progress in which I believed has no future. Worse than that, it dooms the civilization that it is supposed to further.

Its excess will have unfortunate consequences not only on the "developed" countries. In order to enjoy our material comforts, we have created a major risk for the whole of humanity, even for those people who have not benefited in any way from our worthy discoveries. During all these years in which we have promoted – I should say proselytized – the Industrial Way, our attitude has not just been irresponsible; it has also been immoral.

We have created problems for our planet that threaten the survivability of our civilization and our very species. We have built a society that can only survive by growing. If we knew the cause of our irresponsible behavior, we might find a way to remedy it. But we do not. It stems from the very core of our being. Fundamentalism of Progress, insatiability, blind economism and opportunism are not explanations but merely the manifestation of a more profound cause. We can only perceive the meaning of what a human being is today at the philosophical-ontological level.

We forge ahead towards Progress without understanding our real capabilities and limitations. Biologically, we control only the most superficial level of our transient existence and have little control over our faculties, intellectual or physical. We control neither the path of our spermatozoa nor the conception of our children. We do not control the beating of our hearts. We are no better at understanding nature; we do not know for example how trees control their verticality, no more than we know it for ourselves. So, why do not we have the humility to realize how little of life we understand? It is high time that we took stock of our true capabilities so that we can face the future. We can no longer glory in possessing a unique intelligence. Our self-obsession has gone on too long. We are above all a species of animal, rather than an intelligence. And there is no point priding ourselves in being the wisest of the wise (*Sapiens sapiens*). Unwise (*Insipiens*) would be a more accurate term.

We are not genetically "equipped" to live in ego-systems. We cannot ignore that we belong to a real physical world with its gifts and its constraints. The irreparable damage that we have caused to the earth's ecosystem is the mark of the irresponsibility of our species.

In "developed" countries it is almost impossible to escape the unyielding forces of society. It dogs the most private aspects of our lives. Through society, and for society, we have ego-systemized our way of thinking and behaving. The more integrated the individual is into ego-systems, the more irresponsible that same individual acts toward the viability of our species as a whole. The very actions that led to our success are also leading to our downfall.

Industrial society lacks the ability to safely head into the future. By accepting to live in a society that is unsustainable we are living outside the living world. We have lost our sense of duty to life. Our type of civilization is a betrayal of life.

At the very least, prudence demands that we be wary of Western society. It is time that we learned from those societies who have maintained a sustainable way of life and whom we have long, too long, disdainfully called "underdeveloped."

While it is imperative to abandon the *insatiabilis* path on which we are and to search for the *sapiens* path – the path of wisdom – our universities are still tasked with convincing us that we entered the Enlightenment through Reason and that scientific and industrial development will allow the human race to achieve its full potential. Nothing less! Some concerned scientists, aware of the damage that we have inflicted on our planet, claim that we can attain sustainability through good stewardship. Convinced that they are acting positively, their projects remain in the frame of Progress and could be as disastrous as any other industrial development. They still dream of Progress.

The *sapiens* path will not be the path of choice for those who profit most from the ego-systems. Those who industrialize the world usually see every challenge to Development as a hindrance to Progress – a sacrilegious act. Progress is sacred, and cannot be questioned. "You don't stop Progress." To place any restraint on the major corporations is to go against the evolution of humanity. It threatens the economism that is the surest means of finding the sources of money for their investments that will secure the future. It threatens the exploitation of insatiability through which they stimulate consumerism. It threatens the exaltation of the desire for riches that motivates people. It promotes the specter of socialism! And, overall, it threatens the established order.

In short, will Americans, Europeans, Japanese and other people recently embarked on the Train accept to adopt a new course that demands so much self-sacrifice?

This is a critical moment, as critical as the eve of a war for independence, with no margin for error. Today, the independence in question is that of the whole world. Industrial society needs to be liberated from the blind ego-systems that function against the interests of humanity. We will not cure the ills of industrial society without redirecting it.

We are fundamentalists of a Progress that is not consonant with any philosophy of wisdom. Humanity is at stake.

Epilogue

Might we not have forgotten that mankind is a species that belongs to the natural world? Do we still know how to be? How to be a being?

All the paraphernalia with which we enthusiastically surround ourselves and our cybernetic approach to life have turned us into irresponsible creatures. We can progress only by technological development.

Our path is fictive; it leads to the fabled land of opportunity where no human can survive.

If we can collectively free ourselves and rise again as human beings, we might accept to consider the survival of humanity.

Acknowledgments

I would like to thank the persons who have been critically important for this project. They spent hours with me to discuss the manuscript, sometimes page by page. By candidly sharing their perceptions and thoughts on the delicate subject that I wanted to develop, Clayton Berling, Charles Bonner, Henry Chave, Gérard Lévi Alvarès, Ruth Smith, John Stacey, Anne Vanderhoof and Georges Wilson added their touch to this book.

The kindness and talent of Victoria Dare were essential for converting the intricacies of my French into English subtleties.

Caroline Belz, my wife Virginia and my daughters Anne Marie and Catherine were my editors to whom I am more than indebted.

Appendix A

Energy Potentials of Ergamine and Man

Ergamine's potential energy

One ergamine is the thermal potential energy existing in one gram of oil (1/30 once). It is equal to approximately 10 kilocalories (kcal).

Man's potential energy

We can suppose that a man in very good physical condition can shovel 4,000 kg (8,800 lbs) of sand to a height of 1 meter (3.3 feet) per day. In this type of activity, the man's work is to overcome the resistance of gravity. In physics, it can be quantified as follows:

Work = (mass) x (acceleration of gravity) x (height) or:

Work = 4,000 kg x 9.81 m/s^{2*} x 1 m

$\approx$ 40,000 Joules $\approx$ 10 kcal**

This result shows that the daily energy potential of Man and the energy potential of one Ergamine are each roughly equivalent to 10 kilocalories. This is also about 12 Watt-hours, or 0.012 KWH.

This figure is a maximum, as the energy potentials of Man and Ergamine are rarely fully realized in terms of actual labor.

With a work capacity equal to one day's worth of physical labor, the ergamine is an easy unit to use. One ergamine represents one man-day of work; two ergamines represent two man-days, and so on. By analogy, we can extend the notion of the ergamine to all types of energy. Petroleum ergamines, natural gas ergamines, coal, nuclear, hydraulic, wind-powered or geothermic ergamines have all the same potential energy. Each of them can be counted as one servant.

(* 9.81 m/s^2 is the value of the acceleration of gravity)
(** 1 kcal is roughly equivalent to 4,000 Joules)

Appendix B

Energy Conceivable Scenario

How much longer can oil, natural gas, coal and uranium, all of which are finite resources, continue to produce the elixir needed to satisfy the whims of our society; a society which moreover is becoming ever more gluttonous for energy?

Current oil deposits are already showing signs of exhaustion, but it is likely that natural gas deposits will initially make up the shortfall. Oil and gas, the hydrocarbon cohorts that were naturally formed together millions of years ago, will disappear at roughly the same time. How much longer can the two together continue to support industrial society?

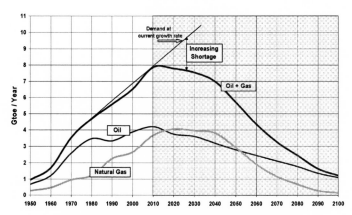

Graph (1): Oil & Gas Global Production

Gtoe = gigatons of oil equivalent per year

Graph (1) shows the quantity of oil and natural gas consumed annually since 1950 and projects the rate of their depletion in future years. The quantities of energy are given in gigatons of oil equivalent per year (Gtoe/yr). One gigaton is equivalent to one billion tons, or one million billion discreet ergamine servants. Because these values are so gigantic, it is very difficult to relate them to our usual measurements. Whichever unit is used, gigatons or billions of ergamines, it is preferable to use them just as markers.

Graph (1) also shows that oil production could peak around 2007-2010 and natural gas production around 2020-2025. Cumulatively, their production could peak between 2012 and 2015. Since 1975, the consumption rate of these two hydrocarbons has been steadily increasing by an average of 2.3% per year. All indications suggest that if the natural deposits of these fuels were inexhaustible and if their use had no negative effects on the environment, they would continue to be consumed at a similar, or even, grater rate in the future. The projected increase in worldwide demand is represented on the graph by the straight line that continues the "Oil & Gas" curve beyond its peak. The explosive Development of South-East Asia and the lightning expansion of global commerce are currently the two main drivers behind this acceleration of energy consumption, and there is no sign of their slowing. After 2010 the natural deposits of hydrocarbons will very probably no longer meet global needs and the global hydrocarbon shortage will become chronic. Year after year, the shortage will only increase.

These forecasts of the global energy situation are however optimistic. They do not take into account the steadily increasing quantities of energy that will be consumed just to extract the hydrocarbons from the ground and to transport them to their places of use. To date the average auto-consumption represents about 7 to 10% of the primary production on the field. These rates can only increase with the depletion of the deposits. According to my own experience, the auto-consumption rate is already in the order of 25% for natural gas brought from the Middle East and Africa to America. It must be carried to the shore in long pipelines where it is liquefied at a temperature of -260°F (-162°C), loaded on methane tankers, transported overseas at this same cryogenic temperature, and then gasified again for consumption. Each of these steps requires a great deal of energy. Likewise, the mining and treatment of oil shale and tar sands today consumes 20 to 50% of the oil that can be extracted from them. The pumping of the last barrels of crude oil from deposits in their final phases of exploitation will require more than 50% of their primary production on site.

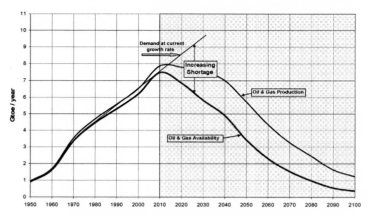

Graph (2): Global Oil & Gas Availability

Gtoe = gigatons of oil equivalent per year

Graph (2) limits the optimism of the previous graph by showing that not all the hydrocarbons produced will actually reach the market. The difference between the curve in Graph (1) (Oil & Gas Production), which has been repeated on Graph (2), and the curve "Oil & Gas Availability" shows the quantity of fuel that is consumed in its extraction, processing and delivery to the market. Graph (2) also shows that after 2010 the "Availability" curve dips even more rapidly than the "Production" curve. This means that the increasing global shortage of hydrocarbons will make our industrialized societies difficult to sustain. By around 2030, the shortage of hydrocarbons could be so great that it would equal their total global production for the year 1970. Even the discovery of new deposits will not alter these forecasts in any appreciable way, and the chances of discovering any significant new hydrocarbon deposits are as slim as those of discovering a new moon orbiting the earth.

Should we go back to coal?

The only fuel that exists in large enough quantities to keep our ego-systems going is the one with which the industrial adventure began: coal. This fuel will now be asked to prevent our extravagant industrial adventure from ending in ruin. Its lack of versatility, however, will considerably reduce its field of application. It will be mainly burned to produce electricity. Large quantities of coal are also likely to be liquefied and turned into a commercial oil product by using processes similar to those used in Germany in World War II and in South Africa during the embargo years following apartheid.

209

The synthetic fuels thus produced would allow us to maintain for only a few years longer our machines that cannot run directly on coal or electricity. This transformation would come at a price: before the synthesized fuel can reach the market, 20 to 25% of the energy contained in the coal itself would be consumed.

Graph (3) introduces coal alongside the hydrocarbons. It shows that its contribution, although sizeable, will in no way allow industrial development to continue its rapid ascent. The graph assumes that the availability of coal will almost double between 1990 and 2030. It is difficult to envisage a greater energy contribution than that because the remaining coal mines will require more and more energy for their exploitation.

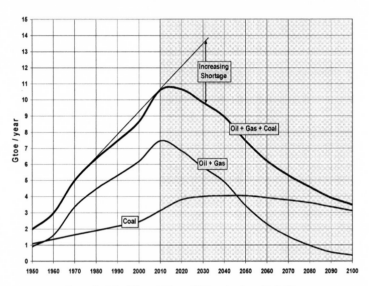

Graph (3): Total Fossil Fuels Availability

Gtoe = gigatons of oil equivalent per year

In Graph (3), the top curve shows the cumulative availability of the three fossil fuels "Oil, Gas & Coal." Even doubling the amount of coal does not reduce in any significant way the energy shortage predicted to begin in 2010; it only pushes back the peak of global depletion of fossil fuels by a few years, from about 2010-2012 to 2015-2017.

What about non-fossil energies? How might these energies help keep our society on its current path? In 2005 total worldwide consumption of all energy sources can be broken down as follows:

FOSSIL ENERGY		83.30 %
Coal	23.80 %	
Oil	31.60 %	
Natural gas	27.90 %	
NUCLEAR ENERGY		5.20 %
RENEWABLE ENERGY		11.50 %
Hydraulic	5.30 %	
Biomass-wood	5.20 %	
Geothermal	0.60 %	
Wind-powered	0.25 %	
Solar-powered	0.15 %	

Graph (4) combines the three types of energy: fossil, nuclear and renewable. For the purposes of this graph it has been assumed that the contributions of nuclear and renewable energies will double between now and 2030. This is a rather optimistic assumption.

The uranium reserves known to date will power our existing nuclear power plants for only another 50 to 60 years. In order to double energy production over the next 100 years, it would thus be necessary, between now and 2050, to multiply fourfold our discoveries of uranium reserves and to build twice more power plants than operate today since those that are currently in operation will have reached the end of their operational life before 2050. These assumptions are bold, to be sure, but are not impossible.

In order to double the share of renewable energies, solar power will have to play a considerably larger role in domestic use. Biofuels will also need to be used extensively, although for the most part they have severe drawbacks.

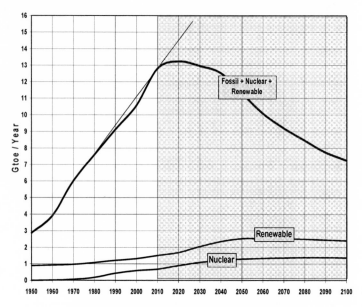

Graph (4): Global Energy Availability

Gtoe = gigatons of oil equivalent per year

Despite the maximum contribution of nuclear and renewable energies, which would involve a doubling of each, Graph (4) shows that the increasing energy shortage, which begins to appear in 2010, is far from closed. It is only slightly reduced. On the other hand, the contribution of these two energies could push back the peak of total energy availability by about 5 years, to 2020. This is a feeble result, especially given the risks associated with the use of nuclear energy. The explosion at the Chernobyl power plant in the Ukraine and the accident at Three Mile Island in Pennsylvania remind us that the industry has not totally mastered the risks involved in operating nuclear power plants. Moreover, it has still not found a reliable means of managing long-lived radioactive waste.

These four graphs show that, no matter which energies are used to make up for the shortage of fossil fuels, 2010 seems to be the fateful date for the beginning of the deficit between demand and supply of energy resources. After 2010, we will enter a period where the market will react in unexpected ways and the industrialized world will be forced to rethink its Development. It will no longer benefit from a plethora of energy but instead face an increasing shortage of energy. This will give rise to other events far more serious than the energy shortage itself and they will force the world, in every way, to slow its pace.

If the scenario on Graph (4) is realized, we would have managed to place an average of about 5,000 ergamines at the service of every individual on earth by around 2020. This massive number of little Cinderellas serving our society demonstrates the extent of Man's social disorder. We should not be surprised that our way of life is unsustainable. Our population is probably ten times too great already and human activity a hundred times too destructive for earth's equilibrium.

After the period 2010-2020, the scenario set out above is of course just a projection and history will reshape the curves presented here. But it would be utopian to think that industrialized societies will act more responsibly in times of crisis than they do in times of plenty. In any case, the energy deficit awaiting the "developed" world after the year 2010 is certain. And it will not be transitory; it will give rise to the greatest chaos that society has ever known. The great energy shortage that awaits us is above all the result of a great lack of foresight by our societies over the last two centuries.

Index

Endnotes

[1] Jean Baudrillard, *Le Pacte de lucidité ou l'intelligence du Mal* (Paris: Galilée, 2004), 14.

[2] Pierre A. Chomat, *Oil Addiction: the World in Peril* (Boca Raton, Florida: Universal Publishers, 2004), 47.

[3] Jean de la Bruyère (1645-1696), "Les caractères ou les mœurs de ce siècle," *Des biens de fortune,* (V) (1688), 35.

[4] Voltaire (1694-1778), *Essai sur les Mœurs et l'Esprit des Nations* (1753)

[5] Edward Bellamy (1855-1898), *Looking Backward, 2000-1887* (Boston, MA: Ticknor, 1888)

[6] Jean-Jacques Rousseau (1712-1778), *Contrat Social,* 1772, Book 1, 8 (Chicago: Encyclopædia Britannica, Great Books of the Western World, Vol. 38, 1952), 393.

[7] Thomas Hobbes (1558-1679), *Leviathan,* 1, 13 (1651)

[8] Jostein Gaarder, *Sophie's World* (New York: Berkley Books, 1997), 133.

[9] Dio Cassius (150-235 CE), *Roman History,* Book 51, 15, 4.

[10] Dominique Quessada, *La société de consommation de soi* (France: Verticales, 1999), 179.

[11] Sean Kay and Theresa Hitchens, *Center for Defense Information* (March-April 2005), 3.

[12] Matter of Scale, *World Watch* (March/April 2004)

[13] Richard Preston, "Climbing the Redwoods," *The New Yorker* (Feb. 14/21, 2005), 214-215.

[14] James Lovelock, *The Revenge of Gaia* (New York: Basic Books, 2006), 6.

[15] Joel Bakan, *The Corporation: The Pathological Pursuit of Profit and Power* (New York: Free Press, 2001), 34 & 37.

[16] John Attarian, *Economism and the National Prospect* (Monterey, VA: American Immigration Control Foundation, 2001), 4 - 5.

[17] Julius Cæsar (100-44 BC), "literally translated" *Cæsar's Commentaries on the Gallic and Civil Wars* (London: George Bell & Son, 1876) Book I, Chap. XV.

[18] Roberta Baskin, "Lobbying is not a hobby," *The Washington Spectator,* Vol. 31, no. 14 (July 15, 2005)

[19] John Perkins, *Confessions of an Economic Hit Man* (San Francisco: Berret-Koehler Publishers, 2004), xi.

[20] Manucher Farmanfarmaian and Roxane Farmanfarmaian, *Blood and Oil* (New York: The Modern Library, 1999), 294.

[21] Pratap Chatterjee, *Iraq, Inc. A Profitable Occupation* (New York: Seven Stories Press, 2004), 179.

[22] Government of United States. Executive Order 13303 of May 22, 2003

[23] World Affairs Council meeting in Monterey, CA (2005)

[24] Michael Parenti, *Against Empire*, (San Francisco, CA: City Light Books, 1995), 46.

[25] Earl Cook, *Man, Energy, Society* (San Francisco, CA: W. H. Freeman and Company, 1976), 414.

[26] John Perkins, *Confessions of an Economical Hit Man* (New York: Plume, January 2006)

[27] Michael Parenti, *Against Empire* (San Francisco, CA: City Light Books, 1995), 35.

[28] *Cluny* (France : MSM, 2004), 39.

[29] *Histoire de l'abbaye de Cluny* (Centre des Monuments Nationaux, 2005)

[30] *Cluny*, "Le véritable philosophe du Christ," (France : MSM, 2004), 150.

[31] Richard Erdoes, *A.D. 1000* (Berkeley, CA: Seastone, 1998), 61.

[32] *Cluny*, (France: MSM, 2004), 97.

[33] Richard Erdoes, *A.D. 1000* (Berkeley, CA: Seastone, 1998), 55.

[34] David Levering Lewis, *God's Crucible, Islam and the Making of Europe, 570-1215* (London: Norton, 2008), 174.

[35] Antoine de Saint-Exupéry (1900-1944), *The Little Prince*, translated from the French by Richard Howard (London: Egmont and Harcourt, 2005), 39-40.

[36] Chris Newbery, Poem "History," *Canticles* (Lexington, KY, 1984), 26.

[37] "Health of the Oceans," *The Ocean Conservancy* (2002 report), 18.

[38] Karen Armstrong, *The Battle for God* (New York, NY: Alfred A. Knopf, 2000), 40.

[39] Ibid, 34.

[40] Alphonse de Lamartine (1790-1869), *Méditations Poétiques*, no. 21, La Foi (1820)

[41] Forbes, "Schwarzenegger seeks to boost hydrogen-fueled cars." http://www.Forbes.com: (accessed September 21, 2005)

[42] United States Department of Energy, Office of Public Affairs (February 18, 2005)

[43] Lester R. Brown, "Supermarkets and Services Stations Now Competing for Grain," *Earth Policy Institute* (July 13, 2006)

[44] Denis Diderot (1713-1784), *Pensées Philosophiques*, no. 18 (1746)

[45] Paul Valéry (1871-1945), *Lettres 1919*, *Œuvres I* (Paris: Gallimard, 1957), 988.

[46] Denis Diderot (1713-1784), *Encyclopédie, ou dictionnaire raisonné des sciences, des arts et des métiers, Pensées sur l'interprétation de la Nature*, no. 15 (1753)

[47] James Lovelock, *The Revenge of Gaia* (New York: Basic Books, 2006)

[48] Dominique Quessada, *La société de consommation de soi* (France : Éditions Verticales, 1999), 23.

[49] Anne Marie Chomat, *Writing in Science* (Wellesley University, 1998), 2, (P.W. Signor 1994, "Biodiversity in Geological Time," *American Zoologist:* 34: 23-32)

[50] USGS, Course 416-350, Chapter 13, Lecture 30: *Non-fuel Mineral Resources* (2005)

[51] *Dictionary of Health*, Vol. 11, Fourth Edition, with Approval and Privilege of the King (Paris: Library of the Duke of Burgundy, M.DCC.LXV), 120-125.

[52] Nathan Smith, Student, University of California at Santa Cruz (2007)

[53] Naomi Klein, "Guns Beat Green: The Market Has Spoken," *The Nation* (December 17, 2007), 10.

[54] Martin Luther King Jr. (1929-1968), speech in Memphis, April 3, 1968.

[55] Descartes (1596-1650), *Discours de la Méthode*, ¹, § 12 (1637)

[56] Karen Armstrong, *The Battle for God* (New York, NY: Alfred A. Knopf, 2000), 69-73.

Printed in the United States
203995BV00002B/1-129/P